CULTURES OF AMERICA

LEBANESE AMERICANS

By Sandra Whitehead

BENCHMARK BOOKS

MARSHALL CAVENDISH

Benchmark Books
Marshall Cavendish Corporation
99 White Plains Road
Tarrytown, New York 10591-9001, U.S.A.

© Marshall Cavendish Corporation, 1996

Edited, designed, and produced by Water Buffalo Books, Milwaukee

In addition to the Lebanese Americans who are named in the text, the author and editors wish to thank the following people whose sharing of knowledge made this book possible: Ghassan Korban, Abid and Maha Arkedan, Ammar Sabsabi, Alixa Naff, and Gregory Orfalea.

Picture Credits: Courtesy of Marshall Arrieh: 23; Sabine Beaupré 1995: 7, 21; © The Bettmann Archive: 11, 12, 13, 15, 17, 20, 70; © Beryl Goldberg: Cover, 1, 4, 40, 42, 51, 52, 57, 58, 73; © Hazel Hankin: 25, 32, 34, 35, 37, 39, 43, 47, 48, 56, 60, 63; © Milwaukee Journal, Ronald M. Overdahl: 54; © Reuters/Bettmann: 19, 75; © UPI/Bettmann: 6, 14, 66, 69; Courtesy of Sandra Whitehead: 5

Library of Congress Cataloging-in-Publication Data

Whitehead, Sandra.
    Lebanese Americans / by Sandra Whitehead.
    p.   cm. -- (Cultures of America)
    Includes bibliographical references and index.
    ISBN 0-7614-0163-6 (lib. bdg.)
    1. Lebanese Americans--Juvenile literature. I. Title. II. Series.
    E184.L34W45   1995   95-11033
    973'.049275692--dc20   CIP

To PS – MS
For Aziz, Ali, Aisha, and Adam Aleiou — SW

Printed in Malaysia
Bound in the U.S.A.

CONTENTS

INTRODUCTION

The first Lebanese immigrants who came to the United States around 1900 did not intend to stay. They thought that, like their ancient ancestors in Lebanon, the Phoenicians, they would leave their beautiful Mediterranean land only briefly, and return with wealth from abroad for their families. But rather than bringing riches back to their families, they brought their families to America, the real treasure they found. Today, almost one hundred years later, about two million Lebanese Americans live in this land of opportunity.

For the early Lebanese immigrants, the United States offered a place where they could make a decent living for their families and practice their religions freely. For later immigrants, it provided a safe haven from a violent, bitter war. For the four generations of Lebanese Americans who have been born in the United States, it is their native land and their home.

As most people do when they move into a home, Lebanese Americans have added their own touches. Just about every major U.S. city has a Middle Eastern restaurant that serves hummus, tabbouleh, and other Lebanese dishes. And pita bread is becoming as common in American homes as Italian loaves. Two generations of Americans grew up with Lebanese American Danny Thomas as their model of an American father, from his popular television series of the 1950s and 1960s, "Make Room for Daddy."

More importantly, Lebanese Americans like consumer advocate Ralph Nader, the Clinton Administration's Secretary of Health and Human Services Donna Shalala, and former Senate Majority Leader George Mitchell are shaping the nation's policies and laws. Such people demonstrate the important contributions Lebanese Americans continue to make to the United States.

A schoolboy in Lebanon holds up the peace sign. Peace is a new experience for Lebanese youth who grew up during Lebanon's civil war, which raged continuously from 1975 to 1991.

CHAPTER ONE

LEAVING A HOMELAND
ESCAPING POVERTY AND WAR

Thirteen-year-old Boutros was as tall as his father, Rachid. The two might have been mistaken for brothers as they walked along the road together in Mount Lebanon in 1918. Mount Lebanon, a mountain range that runs parallel to the eastern coast of the Mediterranean Sea, rises abruptly from a narrow coastal plain. Its sharp cliffs and rocky terrain provided safety to Boutros and his father from both thieves and Ottoman soldiers. Either group might have taken their food or their money.

Boutros grew up fearing the power the Ottoman Turks had over him and his homeland. From 1516 to 1916, Turks ruled Greater Syria, a province of the Ottoman Empire that included today's Lebanon, Syria, Iraq, Israel and other parts of Palestine, and Jordan. (Lebanon was not an independent nation until 1946.)

Boutros's niece Elmaz Abinader describes the last time Boutros and his father traveled together through Mount Lebanon in a memoir that traces the lives of four generations of her Lebanese American family. It was in the spring of 1918, at the end of World War I. They were returning home from buying two steers. It was cold at night in the mountains. As Boutros and his father climbed a rocky path, they turned their faces away from the biting wind.

Modern Lebanon, a nation since 1946, is bordered by Syria, Israel, and the Mediterranean Sea. In the early twentieth century, when about one hundred thousand Lebanese immigrated to the United States, Lebanon was part of the Ottoman Empire's province of Syria.

Boutros's mother had given them her gold bracelets to sell to get money for beef, which was a precious commodity for Boutros's family. During the war, the family rarely ate meat. To do so meant selling off valuable possessions, so instead they grew most of what they ate in their garden. Boutros usually had pita bread with yogurt and onions or figs for dinner.

On the long hike, Boutros listened to his father's tales of travel in South America, stories of encounters with pirates on the Amazon and of his triumphant return to the village as a prosperous, young entrepreneur. At the turn of the century, Boutros's father and two of his uncles had established a rubber trade while living in Brazil, Peru, and Bolivia. Like the Phoenicians, who in ancient times lived in the

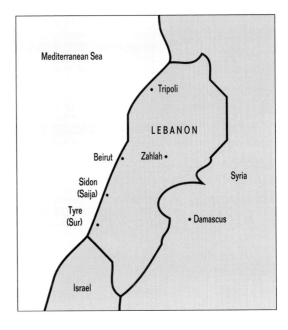

land that is now Lebanon, they had traveled across the sea and returned with treasures from their journeys.

After returning from their beef-buying trip, Boutros often thought of his father's stories. When the war ended later that year, making travel abroad safer, Boutros decided to seek his own fortune in the Americas. It's no wonder that his father's stories inspired Boutros to flee the hardships of life in the mountains of Lebanon. Like other young men in Mount Lebanon at the time, he felt the pressures — religious, political, social, and economic — that led him to leave the white hillsides near Beirut to seek a better life in the United States.

Divided and Conquered

The religious tensions that have existed for centuries in Lebanon are explained in part by the country's history. The borders of today's Lebanon were drawn in 1920, when the French divided what was formerly the Ottoman province of Greater Syria. The French, who had gained control of the province when World War I ended, created the state of Lebanon by combining the largely Muslim-inhabited coast and plain with Christian-dominated Mount Lebanon. Lebanon, which was given its independence from France in 1946, became a nation with an almost equal mix of Muslims and Christians. Druze (a religious group that began as a sect of Shiite Islam but was later considered by many a separate religion) made up about 10 percent of the population.

For practically all of the preceding two thousand years, this territory had been part of larger provinces within great empires: the Ottoman Empire (A.D. 1299-1919), the Islamic (or Arab) Empire (A.D. 630-1250), the Byzantine Empire (the Byzantine Empire existed from A.D. 395-1453, but Byzantine control over Lebanon ended in about 635), and the Roman Empire (64 B.C.-A.D. 395). Since ancient times, Lebanon's location — at the crossroads of Asia, Europe, and Africa — made it an attractive target for conquests. Lebanon's first inhabitants, the Phoenicians, were followed by waves of conquerors, including Assyrians, Persians, Babylonians, and Macedonians under Alexander the Great. Alexander's successors, the Seleucids, ruled the area until 64 B.C., when Pompey conquered it and made it a Roman province.

Religious Tensions

During that long history of domination from outside forces — and still today — the Lebanese people have been divided by their loyalties to their religions and their families. They saw themselves as members of a family and their family as belonging to a particular religious group, rather than to a nation. Each religious community had its own leaders — and sometimes its own militia — much like feudal barons in medieval Europe or China during the early years of the twentieth century, when warlords throughout the country competed for political and economic dominance.

Not only did Muslims, Christians, and Druze compete for political power, but sects within each group also fought among themselves. And within each sect, powerful families often competed with each other to gain control of the group.

Since Muslims came to Lebanon in the seventh century, there has been tension between Muslims and Christians. Although the early Muslims were tolerant of both Jews and Christians as followers of Moses and Jesus (whom they considered prophets), later Muslim rulers began to force the people of Lebanon to accept Islam and speak Arabic. As a result, the Maronite Christians, who had lived in what is

THE GOLDEN AGE OF ARAB CULTURE

When Lebanese Americans consider their heritage, they proudly recall what they consider the golden era of Arab culture, from the eighth to the thirteenth century. During this era of more than five hundred years, the Arab Empire stretched from Central Asia through North Africa to Spain. While Europe was in the Dark Ages, scholars of the Arab Empire were translating Greek and Persian philosophy, studying Indian mathematics and Greek medicine, naming the stars, and developing their own mathematical theories.

Arab poetry and literature also flourished, continuing a tradition started by pre-Islamic Bedouin, who used poetry significantly in daily life. For example, Bedouin poet Aws ibn-Hajar contributed beautiful dirges to be chanted at funerals. Early Arab poetry came in a variety of forms and meters. During the age of the Arab Empire, a poet from what is today's Lebanon, al-Khalil ibn-Ahmad, developed a poetic form that became the norm and continued to be used through the centuries to the present day. The classic prose work *Arabian Nights* (or *The Thousand and One Nights)* was written during this era.

The Arab Empire grew out of the Arab tribes in the Arabian peninsula that united between A.D. 622 and 632 under the Islamic faith. By 633, converts to Islam had reached Greater Syria, an area that included the present-day nations of Syria, Lebanon, Jordan, and Israel. During the next century, they conquered Egypt and all of North Africa, then crossed the Strait of Gibraltar and took the Iberian Peninsula, today's Spain and Portugal. Meanwhile, these Muslims had also gone north to Iran and Iraq and east into India. The Arab

Empire flourished until it began to fragment in the tenth century. Christian Crusaders from Europe and Mongols from Asia captured Arab lands. In the sixteenth century, Ottoman Turks conquered most of the Arab Empire's remaining lands.

Lebanese Christians and Muslims alike are proud of the accomplishments of their ancestors during the Arab Empire. They note the important contribution Arab scholars made to Western culture by introducing Europeans to the works of the ancient Greeks, sparking the European Renaissance. Arab scholars of that era had translated the works of Aristotle and other Greeks into Arabic. The Western world read Aristotle's and Plato's works in Latin translations of Arabic versions. Even after Europe had begun to discover the original works of the ancient Greeks, the Arabic translations proved less remote to Latin scholars than the Greek text. That's because, while ancient Greece seemed distant in time and space, Arab civilization dominated the entire Mediterranean.

Arab contributions to mathematics included the development of algebra and the arabic numeral system still used today. Arab scientists invented the mariner's compass and the astrolabe (used to calculate the position of the stars and planets).

It used to be the prevailing view in Western countries that after the fall of the Roman Empire, the world entered a Dark Age from which it did not emerge until the European Renaissance. However, today we know that while Europe slept, its Arab neighbors were enjoying a brilliant culture based on high religious and moral values, military power, intellectual growth, and economic prosperity.

now northern Syria, fled their homes and established new villages on rugged Mount Lebanon. Mount Lebanon also served as a refuge for minority sects, both Christian and Islamic, who went there to escape oppressors from their own faiths.

The invasion of European Crusaders, beginning in 1097, intensified the strain between Christians and Muslims in Lebanon. Thousands of Maronite Christians fought alongside the Crusaders against the Muslims. The Crusaders gained control of the entire Lebanese coast and Mount Lebanon and kept it for two hundred years. By the late 1200s, the Mamluks of Egypt had driven them out. However, ties were established between the Maronites and the French that have lasted to the present.

As those ties grew stronger, the relationship between Maronites and Muslims deteri-orated. French missionaries founded schools in Maronite communities in Lebanon during the 1600s and 1700s. And even though Lebanon was part of the Ottoman Empire, the French king, Louis XIV, declared that France had the right to protect the Maronites. Trade between the Maronites and the French expanded, and many young Maronite men went to France to study.

All those links with France helped the Lebanese Maronites prosper. They provided a basis for establishing trade relations with the West. Because the Maronites dominated the trade with Europe (a trade that was beneficial to Egypt), the Egyptians, when they occupied Lebanon from 1832 to 1842, gave the Maronites special concessions, such as lower taxes. Muslims, Druze, and other Christians resented the privileges and economic prosperity the Maronites enjoyed.

LEBANON'S RELIGIONS

Religion has always been a central force in both the history of Lebanon and the development of its people's character. Here is a brief discussion of Lebanon's main religious groups.

Islam is one of the great monotheistic religions of the world. (The other two are Christianity and Judaism.) Its followers are called Muslims. Muslims believe that there is one all-powerful God and that His message to the world is revealed in the Koran, the Islamic holy book. The religion's most important prophet, Mohammed, followed a long line of prophets, including Moses and Jesus, who are recognized by Islam.

Muslims are divided into two major sects: Sunni and Shiite. This separation occurred over a dispute about who should have succeeded the prophet Mohammed as the polit-ical leader of Islam. The Shiites believe that Ali, Mohammed's cousin and son-in-law, should have been Mohammed's successor. The Sunnis elected Abu Bakr to take that role.

Lebanese Christians are made up primarily of Maronites, Eastern Orthodox, and Melkites. All three groups are Catholics who are distinguished from each other largely by their use of different liturgies and ceremonies.

The Druze, who separated from the Shiite Muslims in 1019, accept some of the teachings of Islam but have also formed other beliefs and practices. The Druze, considered heretics by both Muslims and Christians for claiming that a *caliph* (the secular and religious head of an Islamic state), al Hakim, was the incarnation of God, moved from Syria to Mount Lebanon for refuge.

When Boutros, the teenager described at the beginning of this chapter, was born in 1905, Mount Lebanon was enjoying a period of political stability. Christians, Muslims, and Druze were living together in peace. Under the Ottoman Turks, they were participating together in a form of self-rule. Even though Mount Lebanon was in the Ottoman province of Syria, it was administered separately from the rest of the province from 1861 to 1915 by an Ottoman Catholic governor appointed directly by Istanbul, Turkey, the capital of the Ottoman Empire. Assisting the governor was an administrative council made up of four Maronite Christians, two Greek Orthodox, one Melkite, three Druze, one Sunni Muslim, and one Shiite Muslim.

That arrangement had been made because of pressures from the French following the massacre of Maronite Christians during a civil war in 1860. Druze in Mount Lebanon and Damascus had attacked Maronite communities and killed ten thousand Maronite Christians after Maronites moved into territories long held by the Druze. The following year, at the insistence of the French, Mount Lebanon was separated from the rest of the Syrian province. Mount Lebanon's governor exerted little control over it, allowing limited self-rule. The Ottoman Turks taxed it at a much lower rate than the rest of Syria. Unlike men in the rest of the province, its young men were not subject to military conscription — the draft — and public security was more or less guaranteed by the French. Mount Lebanon enjoyed its special status until 1915, just before the downfall of the Ottoman Empire in 1918.

During that period of limited self-rule, the Christians on Mount Lebanon became more prosperous. Peasants became land owners, roads were built, schools opened, and trade with the West increased. Naturally, others in the province who did not live on Mount Lebanon envied and resented those who did. A popular saying of the time was "Happy is he who owns so much as a goat's pen on the mountain." Yet, in spite of the peace and privileges they were enjoying, Lebanese Christians never forgot the Druze massacres or their own vulnerability.

The road between Beirut, Lebanon, and Damascus, Syria, is one of the world's oldest and most historic highways. This photo was taken in the early 1900s, when Lebanon was still a part of Syria.

Villages

The divisions between the religious groups of Lebanon were evident in the segregation of its villages. The center of each village was either a church or a mosque, with homes clustered around the church or mosque, like cattle huddling around a tree in a storm. The people living there shared the same faith. In villages where more than one religious group lived, the community was divided along religious lines, with Christians grouping together around their church in one area and Muslims around their mosque in another.

The villagers didn't think in national terms. Their village was their country. When the Lebanese spoke of *baladi,* which means "my homeland," they were referring to their village, not to Lebanon. To Lebanese villagers, towns and other villages seemed like distant countries where different dialects of Arabic were spoken and different religions were practiced. Inside each village, however, people were very intimate with each other. Villagers often even shared blood lines as members of the same extended family. Villagers thus rarely met anyone whose experience of life was much different from their own. Consequently, the pressure to fit in with everyone else was great. Anyone who did not follow the accepted rules of behavior was openly criticized. And any child who tried to misbehave was as likely to be punished by a neighbor as by his or her own parents.

A Common Heritage

In spite of the diverse religions and dialects from one village to another, the life in different villages was really very similar. That was because all Lebanese shared a common Arab heritage that influenced the customs of Chris-

Palestinian women make *sage*, an Arab bread, on a hot iron plate in a Lebanese refugee camp in 1955. Palestinian refugees have lived in Lebanon since 1948, when much of Palestine became the Jewish state of Israel.

BEDOUIN VALUES

When Westerners hear the word "Arab," many of them picture desert nomads on camels. Actually, these nomads, the Bedouins, were the original Arabs. They brought the Arabic language and culture from the Arabian peninsula west to the Fertile Crescent and across North Africa. Many of the values and beliefs of Lebanese Americans and other Arabs were inherited from the Bedouin.

Life in the desert defined their values. Chief among them was loyalty to one's family and the obligation to protect its honor. Nothing worse could happen to a Bedouin than to be disowned by the family and to lose one's tribal affiliation. A tribeless person in the desert had no guarantee of protection or safety.

The importance Arabs place on hospitality comes from traditions formed in the desert. To refuse a stranger food, drink, and a place to rest in the desert could very well mean his or her death. The Bedouin rules of hospitality require a host to shelter and feed a guest, be it a stranger or a friend, for three days, no questions asked.

No greater compliment could be paid to a Bedouin than to call him or her an ideal and generous host. One Bedouin story praises the virtue of Abu Zaid, the mythical hero of the Bani Hillal tribe, who slaughtered his camels one after another to serve their meat to his uninvited guests, until he had no camels left and faced starvation himself.

Other highly valued traits among the Bedouin were individualism and self-reliance. The Bedouin did not want to be beholden to anyone. They did not object to accepting one's hospitality for three days because they could offer to return the favor. However, depending on someone outside of the family for other needs was considered shameful. Children were taught this value through proverbs like "Better a mat of my own than a house shared."

In this 1969 photo, a man wearing traditional Arab clothing (a head scarf and a *galibea*, a long, shirt-like dress) visits Beirut, walking past Lebanese men in western suits. Among the Lebanese, who were strongly influenced by Europeans, suits and ties are the most common men's dress.

tians, Muslims, and Druze alike. This heritage gave them a sense of unity with others who spoke Arabic, in spite of their religious differences.

Arab culture and the Arabic language were brought west from the Arabian peninsula by nomadic Bedouin, many of whom came to the land that is now Lebanon in the seventh century to spread the message of Islam. These Bedouin passed on the values of their heritage in folktales, poetry, and songs that idealized virtues of manliness and honor, individualism and group loyalty, magnanimity and heroism. Even into the twentieth century, the influence of Bedouin values and the Arabic culture can be found in the villagers clothing, family life and values, and relationships within the community.

Clothing. Lebanese villagers dressed modestly and practically. Men and women alike wore comfortable clothing that allowed them to move freely, an asset because their lives were filled with hard work. Women wore blouses and ankle-length skirts. Both Christian and Muslim women usually covered their hair with scarves. For Muslim women, covering their hair was a religious obligation, whereas for Christians, it was a matter of custom.

Men wore collarless white shirts and black pants, called *shirwal,* which were baggy at the hips and the crotch but tapered to the ankles. They also wore a black vest and a sash around their waists. On their heads, they wore a large, square cloth that could be folded in a variety of ways.

Homes. Like clothing, Lebanese houses were simple in the early 1900s. They consisted of small rooms with little or no furniture which either surrounded a small courtyard or opened to the outside. Most homes had dirt floors, but some had slab-stone floors.

During the spring, summer, and fall, the rooms of the house were used primarily for storage, because much of the living was done in the open air. Meals were cooked over a fire. Likewise, when the weather was warm, the families slept outside on mattresses that looked like futons. Sometimes they slept on the flat roof of the house, where night breezes would cool them. When neighbors came to visit, wool rugs were spread on the ground outside for them to sit on.

Every home had a garden, where the family grew grapes, figs, olives, and vegetables. Many families kept a few goats to milk in order to make yogurt and butter. What food they did not produce at home, villagers usually bought in the local marketplace.

Although many homes housed single families, multifamily homes were also common.

The patriarch of a family often had his sons, with their wives and children, sharing his home. Sometimes brothers built a house to share between them. Even in single-family homes, up to three generations often lived together because men usually took in their widowed mothers. Widowed or single sisters also went to live in their brothers' homes when their parents were no longer living.

Family Life. Everyone's role in the family was clear. The father was the head of the household. The eldest son, as he grew older, also shared in his father's tasks and was designated to fill his role in the future. Sons were expected to help support the family when they were old enough to work. Mothers and daughters also worked to bring income to the family, but their chief responsibilities were inside the home. Consequently, sons were more likely to receive an education than daughters. Another reason that daughters in Muslim, Christian, and Druze families alike were not educated beyond the primary grades was so they would not mingle with boys. The families considered it improper for single girls to socialize with boys once they reached puberty.

The mother exerted her authority in the management of the home. This job was considered important and honorable. Women felt fortunate when they did not have to work outside of the home, which took time away from their primary job. However, many peasant women worked in the fields and tended to the animals. Some worked as seamstresses or sold handiwork like knitted or embroidered items. Others worked reeling silk thread from cocoons in the local silk industry.

Daughters were taught from an early age to cook, clean, sew, prepare provisions for the winter, and care for infants and young children. As they grew, they assumed more and more of the chores, freeing the mother from

A Lebanese village woman and her daughter carry water to their home. From an early age, Lebanese daughters help their mothers complete many daily chores.

some of the housework, cooking, and child rearing tasks.

Sons learned their fathers' trade. If the family owned land that could produce crops, men worked to cultivate it. The coastal plain bore tobacco and fruit, including oranges, bananas, grapes, figs, and melons. Cereals and vegetables grew in the fertile Bekaa Valley, which lay to the west of Mount Lebanon. On the mountain, where rainfall is plentiful, apples, cherries, plums, potatoes, and wheat were produced.

Some men raised herds of sheep and goats. Others worked in commerce, especially the Maronite Christians, who had strong ties to the French. Taking advantage of Lebanon's location and its Mediterranean ports, they bought goods from the East and sold them to the West. Some men traded on a smaller scale, peddling wares from village to village in Lebanon and Syria. A few learned trades like carpentry or metal work.

The elder members of the family enjoyed a privileged status. As children grew older, they gradually took on their parents' work, while the parents enjoyed more leisure. When parents became elderly, their sons were completely responsible for supporting them. In addition, respect came with age in Lebanese society. Elder women, as well as men, were treated with honor and had significant say in family decisions. However, the patriarch, the eldest man in the extended family, always had the final say in family decisions.

Family Honor. One's status in the community depended on the reputation of his or her family. The family, more than anything else, gave its individual members their identities. When meeting a stranger, one's first question was often "From whose house are you?" The answer to that question, a family name, usually revealed the person's religion, status, and village or town. Without family, an individual was nobody.

Having a well-respected family in turn brought respect to its members. The reverse was also true. Coming from a family whose reputation was stained would cause difficulties in finding a spouse or a job. Consequently, the family's honor was of utmost importance. Everyone had an obligation to protect it by both avoiding even the appearance of wrongdoing and defending one another against criticism. An insult to a brother or cousin was interpreted as an insult to oneself. Standing up for other family members, even distant relatives, when they were criticized amounted to defending one's personal honor.

Protecting the virtue of women in the family was critical to maintaining the family honor. The entire paternal extended family would be dishonored if a relative became pregnant before she was married. Fathers, brothers, and male cousins shared the responsibility for protecting girls from the possibility of intimacy. Therefore, young women never went anywhere alone. They also were often encouraged to marry as soon as they reached puberty in order to avoid the possibility of becoming an unwed mother. Consequently, at the turn of the century, it was not unusual for girls in their early teens to marry. These limitations on young women were true in Christian, Muslim, and Druze families alike, yet the degree to which they were enforced varied. Muslims and Druze tended to be stricter than Christians.

Having a family member in need was another source of great shame. Families considered it their obligation to take care of each other. To have a relative go outside the family for help or to be reduced to begging would publicly demonstrate that the family had failed in its obligation. Members of the extended family were intimately aware of relatives' needs because of the close relationship they enjoyed. If family members were sick or needed money, relatives would rally to help.

Community Life. Like family, neighbors also provided each other with support and fellowship. Village women would often lighten the burden of preparing food supplies for winter by working together with their neighbors. They shared stories while stringing vegetables for drying or bundling grape leaves before preserving them in salt water. The grape leaves would be used throughout the year to make *yubbra,* rolled grape leaves with rice, meat, and spices inside.

Neighbors also shared the chore of preparing wool for bedding. After the sheep were sheared, the wool was washed by hand and then laid out to dry in the sun. Once it was dry, women fluffed it by beating it with sticks.

Then they carefully pulled it apart by hand to make sure no burrs were left. Finally, they stuffed the wool into large bags made from heavy cloth to make mattresses. Such chores were made less tedious by making them a social occasion.

Numerous ceremonies also created occasions for socializing. Engagements, marriages, births, Christian baptisms, and Christian and Muslim religious holidays were celebrated with feasting and visiting. Upon arriving at a celebration, men and women usually went into separate parties. Someone would bring out a *derbekki,* a ceramic drum with leather stretched across the top, and provide a beat for dancing. A woman or two would stand up and dance. Everyone would cheer and clap. The traditional cry of celebration would ring out: *"La, la, la, la . . . leeeeesh!"* Then the dancer would sit down to let another have a turn. Likewise, the men would do their own dancing in another room.

Although women's socializing was limited to such celebrations and to visits with neighbors, men also gathered at coffeehouses with friends. There they drank thick Turkish coffee and smoked *arghilehs,* Turkish water pipes. Some played backgammon. Men also enjoyed strolls through the village and the marketplace. When women went for walks or to the market, they were accompanied by a male member of the family.

Hard Times on the Mountain

Life on Mount Lebanon was difficult, in spite of its political stability and relative prosperity. Its rocky soil and sharply sloped terrain limited farming. Even though villagers had cultivated every bit of land possible, they were still

These women are performing a traditional dance at a performance in Beirut. In traditional gatherings, Lebanese women and men dance in separate groups.

unable to produce enough to feed themselves. They depended on imports for much of their food staples.

Land shortages were made worse by an increasing population. Families on Mount Lebanon tended to be large. Fast population growth caused overcrowding and contributed to food shortages. When children grew up and were ready to establish their own households, only one of them could inherit the family farm. With no other land available, some decided to move out and seek homes elsewhere.

Of those who did inherit the farm, many found that they could not make a living through farming alone. For this reason, home industries developed. People worked at home industries like spinning, weaving, and silk reeling (winding silk thread from cocoons onto spools).

During the first half of the nineteenth century, silk was Mount Lebanon's chief export. Villagers cultivated silkworms to produce raw silk that was sold to Europeans for textiles. The

THE CEDARS

The cedar tree, with its strong wood and spreading branches, is a long-standing symbol for Lebanon. Today it appears on the Lebanese flag, on coins, and sometimes on postage stamps.

Since ancient times, the people of the area have held the cedar in high regard. The Bible sings its praises in Psalms 104:16, saying, "The trees of the Lord are full of sap; the cedars of Lebanon, which he hath planted. . . ."

Long ago, majestic cedars covered the mountains of Lebanon. Solomon, a king of ancient Israel, used them for timber to construct his temple, the Phoenicians used them to build ships, and the Egyptians built palaces with them.

After centuries of cutting, only a few are left. Today, a protected grove of about four hundred cedars stands near the top of a mountain in the northern part of the Mount Lebanon range.

---

silk reelers' success ended when the Suez Canal opened in 1869, bringing competition from East Asia. The opening of the canal made purchasing Chinese silk less expensive than it had been, and Europeans preferred it to the coarser silk made it Mount Lebanon, considering it to be of higher quality. The decline of the silk industry had a devastating effect on some families and even whole villages that depended on it as their primary source of income.

Starvation and Oppression

When the Ottoman Turks entered World War I in 1914 on the side of the Central Powers (Germany, Bulgaria, and Austria-Hungary), life on Mount Lebanon became more difficult. The Ottoman military confiscated already-short wheat supplies for the army. Allied fleets blockaded the coasts, preventing foodstuffs, medical supplies, and clothing from being imported. Soon famine spread throughout the province of Syria, hitting Mount Lebanon particularly hard. Gregory Orfalea, of Los Angeles, recalls his grandmother telling him how, as a child, she watched her two younger brothers starve to death on Mount Lebanon while their mother went from village to village trying to get them food. Historians estimate that as many as one-fourth of the entire mountain population died from starvation and sickness during the war years, from 1914 to 1918.

Survivors told stories of people starving in the streets while others searched through garbage for lemon or orange peels to eat. Some people are said to have sold their lands and homes for small quantities of food. Others who had nothing to sell took to stealing food. As a result, young men spent many evenings outside, guarding the family's fields.

By 1916, famine, overcrowding, successive swarms of locusts, and epidemics (including typhoid, malaria, and bubonic plague) had brought much suffering to Mount Lebanon. To make matters worse, the Ottoman Turks were drafting some young Lebanese men to fight for them in World War I. Conscription fell heaviest on Muslims and Druze. Residents of Mount Lebanon, who were primarily Christian, were exempt from the draft, and Christians in other parts of the province escaped through emigration or by moving to Mount Lebanon. For Lebanese families, the draft meant not only separation from a loved one, but also the loss of an important bread winner.

Political oppression was also a problem during the war. The dying Ottoman Empire lashed out against Arab nationalists, hanging patriots in Lebanon who had been conspiring to end Ottoman rule. After the war, many

Lebanese people, who had been promised independence by the Allies (the United States, Britain, France, Russia, and Italy), felt betrayed when they found themselves under French control.

Rumors of a Land of Plenty

As difficult as their lives were, the Lebanese would probably have stayed put had it not been for the promise of a better life in the West. And so, when early emigrants returned home with stories and evidence of the wealth that could be found abroad, "American fever" struck.

Villagers in Baskinta, high in the Mount Lebanon range, caught the fever when a letter arrived from a former villager who had left to peddle goods in the United States. Betrus Saad, who emigrated to the United States in 1888, sent two hundred dollars to his brother after peddling for three years. The story is told that the same day the money and letter arrived, word of his success spread and forty young men from his village departed to seek their fortunes in the United States.

More widespread were stories told by Lebanese Christian tradesmen and merchants who had exhibited goods at the Philadelphia International Exposition in 1876, the Chicago Fair of 1893, and the St. Louis Fair of 1906. They returned from those expositions and told of the great success they had selling religious curios from Lebanon, the Holy Land. Stories of skyscrapers, electricity, streetcars, and hot and cold running water must have sounded unbelievable to villagers who heard them. Such stories inspired a wave of would-be merchants to pack their bags and head for the United States.

The Lebanese's impressions of the United States were further enhanced by American Protestant missionaries who had opened numerous schools in Lebanon in the nine-

Lebanese children sit on their balcony in Beirut in 1990, only months before the end of the civil war in Lebanon. Their home is on Beirut's Green Line, the scene of constant fighting during the war.

teenth century. In 1866, missionaries started the renowned American University of Beirut, formerly called the Syrian Protestant College. Contact with the missionaries and the education they offered sparked the interest of Lebanese youth in the missionaries' homeland.

With great expectations, Lebanese families decided to send their sons to the United States. Most of them intended to work for a few years, then return to Lebanon with enough money to buy a house or a store. Little did they know that few of them would actually return.

Early twentieth-century immigrants arrive at Ellis Island in New York. Each immigrant had to pass an inspection on the island before being granted permission to stay in the United States.

CHAPTER TWO

LIFE IN A NEW LAND
THE LEBANESE COME AND STAY

Najeeb Arrieh was fifteen when he came to the United States in 1906. He came to the United States to find an opportunity to work and to make a decent living. Like many other early Lebanese immigrants, Najeeb did not plan to stay. There just were not many opportunities for young men to work in Mount Lebanon while it was under oppressive Ottoman rule.

Najeeb's parents considered financing his journey as a family investment. They sent him to live with his uncle, who had settled in Milwaukee, in a community begun by Lebanese immigrants who had participated in the Chicago Fair of 1893. He would make about fifteen dollars a month selling fruit from his uncle's stand, sending what he could back to his family. But Najeeb's father made him promise to return home after three years. He did not want to lose his eldest son.

The First Wave of Lebanese Immigrants

Najeeb came to the United States during the first big wave of Lebanese immigration.

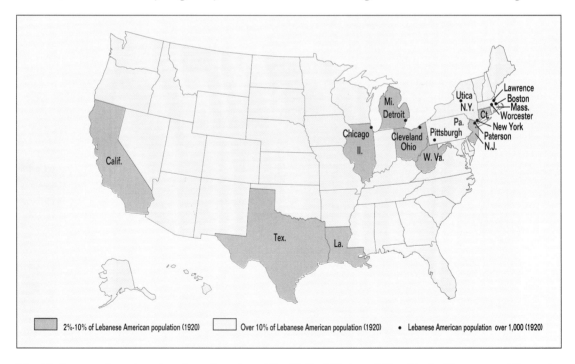

Most Lebanese American immigrants entered the United States at New York. They spread throughout the country, with the largest Lebanese communities in the northeastern and northern Midwest states.

From 1881 to 1925, about one hundred thousand Lebanese came to the United States. Although they made up a small portion of the twenty-seven million immigrants who came to the United States during that period, they represented about one-fourth of the population of Lebanon. Most of the Lebanese immigrants were Christians from Mount Lebanon. By 1891, every village on Mount Lebanon could claim at least one immigrant son in America.

The first wave of immigration from Lebanon peaked in 1914, on the eve of World War I, with about nine thousand Lebanese coming here that year. The difficulties of travel during the war practically stopped Lebanese from immigrating until the war ended in 1918. By 1921, immigration from Lebanon was up again to about five thousand a year. However, it tapered off after 1921 because of new U.S. immigration laws that set quotas on the number of immigrants allowed from each country.

Making an Entrance

Like most of the early immigrants to the United States, the Lebanese entered the country through Ellis Island in New York Harbor, near Manhattan. The Lebanese called the island *"bayt al-hurriyah,"* meaning "the house of freedom." After passing an immigration inspection in one of its huge, red brick buildings, newcomers were free to begin their pursuit of happiness.

Fears of being denied entry were so strong that many immigrants considered the trek through the immigration inspection almost as treacherous as the hazardous sea voyage they had just made. Whole families sometimes waited on Ellis Island for days, even weeks, while one member was observed in the island's infirmary for signs of contagious disease. One young man, afraid that his fourteen-year-old sister would be returned because of her glaucoma, smuggled her through wrapped in a carpet slung over his shoulder.

Widespread Settlement

Once they passed through customs, the immigrants usually met supportive relatives waiting to help initiate them in the ways of their new home. Relatives provided a place to

ANTONIOS BISHALLANY: THE FIRST LEBANESE IMMIGRANT

Antonios Bishallany is said to be not only the first Lebanese, but the first Arab, to immigrate to the United States. What pushed him to leave Lebanon in 1854 was a desire to expand his religious education.

The teachings of American Protestant missionaries had impressed him, so he traveled to the United States to pursue his religious studies. This made him an exception, because most immigrants were more interested in coming to find work.

In his early twenties, Bishallany sold everything he owned and sailed for the United States. After a two-month voyage, he arrived in Boston. Then he went straight to New York to seek people he had met when he served as their tour guide in the Holy Land. He got a job with one wealthy family on Fifth Avenue as its butler. Soon he began exchanging Arabic lessons for English lessons. In the fall of 1855, he began his studies at a seminary in Duchess County, New York.

But, just a year later, his sojourn in America came to a tragic end. By the fall of 1856, before his dream of becoming a minister could be realized, he had died of tuberculosis.

stay and work. Early ethnic organizations that were formed around religious groups also offered newcomers support and a ready group of friends. Likewise, Lebanese American churches aided new immigrants and provided opportunities for fellowship.

Like Najeeb, most of these immigrants planned to work in the United States for a few years, then return home with money for their families. Because they did not plan to stay, most of them were not particular about where they lived, as long as there was an opportunity to work. The vast majority of the first Lebanese immigrants scattered throughout the country, working as peddlers. Some moved to industrial centers to work in factories. Lebanese pioneers ventured to New York, Boston, Detroit, Chicago, Houston, Birmingham, and Los Angeles with the hope of making some quick profits.

In most places, the Lebanese immigrants moved into neighborhoods with other immigrants — Irish, Jews, Poles, and Russians. Because their numbers were relatively small, compared with other immigrant groups, the Lebanese posed no threat. So they usually lived peacefully together. Occasionally, friction developed between the immigrant groups because of differences over the Catholic faith. Some tiffs between the Lebanese and the Irish were reported in New York newspapers, which also noted that clergy intervened, reminding both sides to act like members of the Christian family to which they belonged.

Because of the early immigrants' willingness to go where the jobs were, Lebanese Americans can be found throughout the United States today. Although most Lebanese Americans today live on the eastern seaboard, a large number of them live in the Midwest, most notably in Detroit-Dearborn, Cleveland, Chicago, and Toledo. Today Detroit has surpassed New York

James (Najeeb) Arrieh, who immigrated in 1906 when he was fifteen, poses next to a car bearing the name of his food store in Milwaukee. Like many Lebanese immigrants, he got his start peddling someone else's goods, then earned enough money to open a store of his own.

as the U.S. city with the largest Lebanese American population, with more than 125,000 Lebanese Americans. Strong Lebanese American communities are also found in the South and West. And a growing number of Lebanese Americans are moving to southern California, where the climate and landscape resemble the Mediterranean shores of Lebanon.

Lebanese Americans are also found in the country's smaller cities and towns. The Lebanese immigrants were more willing than other immigrant groups to branch out from the urban areas and establish themselves in communities where few other Lebanese lived. Consequently, large Lebanese American communities are found in upstate New York and smaller cities surrounding Chicago, Los Angeles, Boston, Dallas, and other urban centers.

From Visitors to Settlers

For several years, Najeeb worked for his uncle, selling fruits and vegetables. He eventually saved enough to open his own store, in spite of sending money to his family regularly. In 1917, when he was twenty-three, Najeeb married his cousin, who had come from Lebanon to keep house for her three brothers. Like other Lebanese immigrants, he decided to take an American name when he became a citizen. He adopted the name James. Two world wars and the Great Depression interfered with his plans to return to Lebanon. Forty years passed before he made it back, long after his mother and father had died, and then he went just for a visit.

Najeeb's experience was played out by hundreds of other Lebanese immigrants around the country. In spite of their intentions to return to Lebanon, most of the immigrants ended up staying here.

However, some immigrants came with the intention of staying from the start. One of them was twelve-year-old Regina Abounamy. Regina saw coming to the United States as the chance to finally have plenty to eat, nice clothes, and an education — things not available to her at the turn of the century in Aitannet, the village where she lived on Mount Lebanon.

Her parents sent her to the United States in 1908 with her aunt and uncle. They had a relative, a wholesaler of dry goods, who had promised to help them get started as peddlers. She had not peddled long before she decided

she would prefer the security of work in a garment factory to the peddler's life on the open road. She moved in with other immigrants on Washington Street in Lower Manhattan and found work in a factory.

About the same time, Habib Shuhda, an expert silk weaver from Homs, Syria, who had found work in a silk mill in Hoboken, New Jersey, finally made enough money to open his own shop. He and a relative bought a dry goods store together on Washington Street. He also had a small stand for selling roasted nuts and seeds that later turned into a profitable wholesale business.

Regina met Habib in his store. Their interest in each other soon grew into love, and they married when she was nineteen and he was thirty-five. The couple worked together in the store and participated in Washington Street's lively Lebanese American community. Washington Street, with its dry-goods stores and immigrant banks, was a mecca for peddlers in the beginning of the twentieth century.

It was also one of the few old-country Lebanese communities in the United States. A Middle Eastern bazaar had been transplanted there, complete with Turkish coffee houses, rug-weaving factories, and groceries full of Middle Eastern spices. New York, and Washington Street particularly, became the leading business, cultural, and intellectual center for Lebanese Americans and remained so until after 1948, when Detroit gained that position.

Habib and Regina attended the Washington Street's *haflis,* parties that featured Arabic musicians playing the *oud,* an Arabic instrument similar to a mandolin, and included Arabic food, dancing, and plenty of singing. Haflis, newspapers written in Arabic, and the bakeries that made *halloweeat,* which were Lebanese desserts like *baklawa* (a pastry filled with sugar

Sahadi's Delicatessen, on Atlantic Avenue, is a popular store in the Arab section of Brooklyn. For the early Lebanese immigrants, New York was the center of economic and cultural life.

and nuts and topped with a lemon-honey syrup), reminded Regina of her native land. Her heart was always in Lebanon, but there was no life for her there under the cruel control of the Ottoman Turks, explained her son, Joseph Shuhda of Brooklyn.

Forty-six years after she immigrated, Regina finally visited Lebanon in 1954. Habib had died two years earlier. When Regina got there, she did not recognize her mother. Her father had died the year before she returned, and she met her younger sister for the first time. After two months there, Regina returned to the United States, a place that had truly become her home.

Peddling

Because most of the early Lebanese immigrants wanted to save money to take back to Lebanon, they were extremely frugal. They usually lived in cramped quarters, sleeping on floors in rooms without heat or running water.

In that regard, the Lebanese were like many other immigrant groups. What distinguished them was their choice of occupation: peddling. No other immigrant group, with the exception of German Jews, so completely identified with peddling as a line of work. Historians estimate that before 1914, at least 90 percent of the Lebanese immigrants, including women and children, took up peddling, if only for a short time.

Some, like Najeeb, sold goods from carts on street corners or went door-to-door. The most typical peddlers, however, traveled from town to town with heavy suitcases strapped to their backs and smaller cases, called *kashshi,* strapped to their chests. The kashshi were filled with "notions" — small, useful items like scissors, razors, pins, and buttons. These peddlers also carried satchels in each hand. Peddlers often dedicated one satchel to items they said were from the Holy Land, like crucifixes, rosaries, and Eastern Orthodox icons, which were pictures or statues of saints or other religious symbols that were themselves considered sacred. (Most of these items were said to have been manufactured in New York.) One third-generation Lebanese American from Los Angeles, Gregory Orfalea, recalls that when he asked his grandmother, who came in 1893 and peddled notions all over the eastern seaboard, how she managed to offer holy water from her notions case, she proclaimed, "Why, I blessed it myself."

The peddling life was hard. Some peddlers were on the road for up to six months. Orfalea, who spent years researching the Arab immigrant experience, talks of hearing "tales of women whose frozen skirts cut their ankles, of blackened, frostbitten faces, and of men sleeping in buggies who froze to death by morning."

Why would they choose such a hard life? One reason was money. Hard-working peddlers made a lot of money. Lebanese peddlers are reported to have made about $1,000.00 a year, about three times the average U.S. income in 1910 (which was $382.00), four times that of the American farmer, and slightly less than twice the income of a factory worker, a coal miner, or a salesperson in a shop.

In addition to the profits, early Lebanese immigrants were attracted to peddling by the freedom and self-reliance it offered. The Bedouin values Lebanese Americans inherited placed great importance on being the master of one's own destiny. Consequently, many Lebanese Americans chose peddling over the factory jobs that so many immigrants from other countries used as stepping stones to the middle class.

Peddling gave Lebanese Americans more than money. It gave them a quick initiation into American life. When traveling from farm house to farm house, hawking lace, ribbons, and religious trinkets, the new immigrants quickly learned English. This helped them get ahead in the United States faster than some of the other ethnic groups, who clustered in well-established communities that looked much like the old country. In addition to learning English, Lebanese peddlers saw this country and met its people. They learned American customs and gradually adopted the American lifestyle.

The Peddlers' Network

The old Arab proverb, "Trade will lead a man far," proved to be true of the Lebanese peddlers in the United States. The father of famous American disc jockey Casey Kasem left Mount Lebanon in 1895 and peddled through South America and Mexico before settling in the United States. Like the elder Kasem, other Lebanese peddlers also covered lots of ground.

A network of peddling settlements sprang up across the nation from New York to Los Angeles and from Minneapolis to New Orleans. These communities served as hubs for peddlers, a place from which they would stock up and head out. New immigrants came from Lebanon, some with only the name of a city and a supplier they planned to contact. Often they did not even know where the city was. With the help of other Lebanese immigrants, they eventually found their suppliers. Once they did, the new immigrants were given their peddling packs and sent out on the road the same day.

The End of the Peddling Era

Peddling as an occupation began to fade by 1910. The peddlers became small shop owners. Many of them went on to own bigger stores. Some of them even became millionaires. Two of the most successful Lebanese immigrants made their fortunes selling men's apparel: Mansour Farah and Joseph Marion Haggar.

Farah immigrated from Mount Lebanon in 1905. After working in a store with his brother, Farah decided to go to New York to study shirt design and manufacturing. Then he moved to El Paso, Texas, where he opened a small factory that made work shirts. The business grew steadily, and he started producing jeans and overalls. When he died in 1937, his sons took over the business. Under their leadership, the Farah Company expanded further, even winning a contract to make khaki clothing for the U.S. Army in World War II.

Joseph Marion Haggar's famous Haggar slacks have made him the world's largest manufacturer of men's dress slacks today. Haggar, who immigrated in 1908 when he was seventeen, spent a number of years as a traveling peddler, selling men's overalls. In 1926, when he had enough money to start his own business, he moved to Dallas. There he opened his own factory for manufacturing work pants. His assembly-line approach to making clothes became a model for the industry.

Another successful businessperson was Ameen Haddad. He moved from a fruit stand to a highly successful potato farming and wholesale business. He was known as the "potato king" by others in the produce business.

Lebanese Laborers

Not all Lebanese immigrants peddled wares for a living, particularly Lebanese Muslims who began immigrating at the end of the peddling era, after 1910. Muslims, many of whom found work in factories, were slower to come to the United States because they did not have the Western ties that Lebanese Christians did. Also, some Muslims were reluctant to come to a Christian country, where they were afraid it might be hard to practice their faith. Some Lebanese Christians also found work in factories. Although most Lebanese did not want to work as laborers, factory work lured them with the promise of quick cash. Because many of them were uneducated and did not speak English, it was one of the few occupations open to them.

Many Lebanese immigrants found jobs right after they got off the boat, working in textile mills and the garment industry in New York City and Paterson, New Jersey. Others moved to New England to work at the cloth mills in Lawrence and Fall River, Massachusetts, then the wool and cotton centers of the world.

Work in the mills was not easy. The mills were literal sweatshops. Inside they felt like steamy ovens. Steam was used to keep threads from snapping. The vibration of the looms made a deafening noise. And pay for garment workers was terribly low — ten dollars a week for men and about half that for women.

Other Lebanese laborers took jobs in factories in America's growing industrial centers. Because labor shortages were a persistent problem for the rapidly growing industries in the early twentieth century, Lebanese who were willing to work in factories could always find jobs. These workers were usually well paid and, therefore, able to move into the economic middle class rather quickly.

Some Lebanese immigrants found work in steel mills in Pittsburgh and Birmingham. But the biggest community of Lebanese laborers was in Detroit, where work on automotive assembly lines employed many Lebanese immigrants. At the turn of the century, Detroit had only 50 Lebanese Christians, mostly single men. By 1916, 555 Lebanese men, Christian and Muslim, were working at the Ford car plants.

The "Asian" Controversy

Wherever they found work, Lebanese Americans usually felt fairly welcome. Because of their relatively small numbers, early Lebanese immigrants did not encounter the same degree of prejudice that the Irish, Jews, Mexicans, Italians, and other ethnic groups did. There was no ethnic slur like "mick," "kike," "dago," or "wop" for this group. Sometimes they were treated with animosity when they were mistaken for Turks because Turkey was an enemy of the United States in World War I. In those cases, most Lebanese did not take offense because they realized the anger they met was not really directed at them.

On the other hand, as foreigners, the early Lebanese immigrants faced the same prejudice and discrimination that all foreigners did in the United States early in the twentieth century. As increasing numbers of non-Europeans immigrated to the United States, a wave of antiforeign prejudice swept over the country. Because the Lebanese, with their baggy pants and their olive skin, looked more foreign than most European immigrants, they sometimes met more racism than other non-European immigrants did.

In part because of Lebanese Americans' appearance, and possibly because Lebanon, although a Middle Eastern nation, is actually on the western edge of the Asian continent, many Americans considered Lebanese to be Asian. In the early twentieth century, many white Americans of European descent held strong prejudices against Asians. They looked down on Asian immigrants as inferior and feared they would dilute the racial purity and weaken the moral fiber of the nation. Those attitudes resulted in immigration laws that discriminated against Asians.

These laws affected Lebanese Americans in 1910, when the U.S. Census Bureau classified them as "Asiatics," one of the bureau's racial classifications for use on census forms. The following year, the Bureau of Immigration and Naturalization ordered court clerks to reject immigration applications from "aliens who were neither white persons nor persons of African birth and descent," and Lebanese began to be disqualified for citizenship.

Costa George Najour, who was from Mount Lebanon, contested the denial of his citizenship request. The Lebanese community in New York, led by the Arabic press, rallied the Lebanese in the country and raised one thousand dollars to appeal the decision. On appeal, the Lebanese were proclaimed white persons within the meaning of the naturalization laws.

Although this case was resolved, others arose in the southern and midwestern states. The controversy mobilized Syrian and Lebanese organizations throughout the country. The Society of Syrian National Defense organized and vowed to "fight to the death to defend the rights and honor of all who speak Arabic and are born under Asian skies." One lawyer who defended a Lebanese immigrant whose citizenship request had been denied argued that if Syrians (as the Lebanese were then called) were Asian, then Jesus, who was born in Syria, was Asian. He won the case. Other Lebanese won their cases as well, and the "yellow race" issue gradually disappeared. The Immigration Act of 1917 made the issue moot when it made it illegal to deny someone citizenship on the basis of race.

ARAB STEREOTYPES

Radio personality Casey Kasem, the most prominent Druze Lebanese American, tells the story of how his son, Mike, then twelve, walked into the living room one day and told him, "Dad, I hate Arabs."

Kasem, a Lebanese American, was shocked. When he asked Mike why, his son told him because of what he saw in movies and on television. Unfortunately, the term "Arab" has taken on a number of negative connotations, says Kasem.

Since they first came to the United States at the turn of the century, Lebanese Americans have been confronted with Arab stereotypes. Many of those stereotypes have been influenced by media portrayals of Arabs.

Since the 1920s, there have been films, cartoons, and television shows portraying Arabs as womanizers, buffoons, and bearded killers. Arab stereotypes even appeared in silent films, like Rudolph Valentino's 1921 movie *The Sheik*. In it is the memorable line, "When an Arab sees a woman he wants, he takes her." Bob Hope and Bing Crosby were chased across the desert by sword-wielding Arabs in the popular 1942 comedy *The Road*

to Morocco. Dustin Hoffman and Warren Beatty remade the film in 1987 with similar characterization and titled it *Ishtar.* (Perhaps as a form of justice, the movie died at the box office.)

In the 1970s, when long lines formed at U.S. gas stations to buy expensive gas that was being rationed because of an agreement made by the major oil-producing countries, Arabs became popular villains. The cartoon image of an oil-rich sheik wearing dark glasses covered with dollar signs became common.

Other Arab villains have included "mean" wrestlers on televised wrestling programs that wear an Arabic headdress and have names like "The Sheik" or "Abdullah." More recently, U.S. films have often portrayed Arabs as terrorists.

What is missing, Kasem says, is a positive portrayal of Arab Americans that more closely depicts reality. The exception was Lebanese American Danny Thomas, who portrayed a very likeable character in his television shows in the 1950s and 1960s. However, he was always identified as a Lebanese rather than as an Arab.

Fueled mainly by competition for jobs, anti-immigrant feelings flared again during the Great Depression, and Lebanese, like other immigrants, again faced prejudice. But when prosperity returned, so did friendly relations. Since then, Lebanese Americans have mostly enjoyed good relationships with other Americans, only occasionally marred by American anger toward Arabs over events in the Middle East.

Fitting In

In fact, according to some historians, second-generation Lebanese Americans fit in so

well with American society that they were in danger of completely assimilating, or disappearing into the general population. In the 1920s, when the second-generation Lebanese Americans were coming of age, many of their immigrant parents were more interested in their children being accepted and succeeding in American society than in maintaining their cultural heritage.

Second-generation Lebanese American Marshall Arrieh, the son of Najeeb Arrieh, who was introduced in the beginning of this chapter, says that maintaining his Lebanese identity has been "an uphill battle." As a successful lawyer, he found himself welcomed into the U.S. mainstream. But as a self-defined "traditionalist," he has worked to keep Lebanese culture in his family. Although many Lebanese Americans of his generation married outside the ethnic group, he married another second-generation Lebanese American, Victoria. They attend a Melkite church, one of the denominations Lebanese immigrants brought to the United States, and eat Lebanese food at home.

Like many second- and third-generation Lebanese Americans, however, the Arriehs don't speak Arabic at home. Marshall studied Arabic when he was a student at Princeton University and continues teaching it to himself. But his five children know only a few words.

Many second- and third-generation Lebanese Americans have also adopted American lifestyles, sometimes replacing Lebanese customs with American ones. In an effort to maintain the Lebanese heritage in his family, Marshall has taken his wife and children to Lebanon to partake of Lebanese culture first-hand. Life in the United States is so busy that it's impossible to experience the relaxed rhythm of the Lebanese lifestyle here, he says.

The Second Wave of Lebanese Immigrants

The second wave of immigration from Lebanon began after the 1967 Arab-Israeli War and has continued to the present. Emigration from Lebanon and the surrounding Arab countries increased markedly after Israel defeated Egypt, Syria, and Jordan in the Six Day War of 1967. Immigration from Lebanon has increased even more since the Lebanese civil war began in 1975. Of the more than two million Lebanese Americans

THE LEBANESE CIVIL WAR

Civil war in Lebanon, from 1975 to 1991, drove many Lebanese to leave and seek a better life elsewhere. More than forty-three thousand Lebanese immigrated to the United States during the war.

The war began when fighting broke out between Lebanese Muslims and the Phalange party, a political group dominated by Christian Maronites, for control of the country. The war also involved Syria, Israel, and the Palestinian Liberation Organization (PLO), the political leaders of the Palestinian people. Each of these groups was fighting in Lebanon for its own purposes.

The PLO had established bases in Lebanon for fighting Israel. In 1978, Israel invaded southern Lebanon in order to drive out the Palestinians. In 1982, it invaded again, overrunning the PLO. Israeli troops remained in southern Lebanon. Syria had also intervened against the PLO, bringing Lebanon largely under its control.

The Lebanese people were caught in the cross-fire of the various armies and militias. The Shiite Muslims of southern Lebanon found their homes, villages, and farms destroyed by Israelis who were attacking Palestinian bases there in retaliation for Palestinian attacks on Israel. Tens of thousand of Shiites were forced to flee southern Lebanon.

Beirut, the capital of Lebanon, which had often been called the "Paris of the Middle East" for it's beauty and sophistication, was reduced to rubble by fighting between the Christian and Muslim factions. Most of the fighting ended in 1991, when a peace agreement was hammered out.

in this country, more than fifty-six thousand have come here since 1967, including about forty-three thousand who came since 1975.

Unlike the Lebanese immigrants of the first wave, second-wave immigrants were part of larger Arab immigration. First-wave Lebanese immigrants were almost the only Arabs coming to the United States at that time, whereas second-wave Lebanese immigrants were joined by Arabs from twenty-two countries. For about seventy years, Lebanese Americans dominated the Arab American community, but today they are part of a community that is made up of Arab people from diverse national origins.

Escaping War

Many Lebanese of the second wave of immigration came here because they found life unbearable during their country's civil war. Many people left Lebanon during the war years. Some of them went to North and South America, Europe, Africa, other Arab countries, and even as far away as Australia. Most of them planned to return once peace was restored. As Ibrahim Mortada found out, this was not easy.

A Shiite Muslim from Tyre, a city on Lebanon's southern Mediterranean coast, Ibrahim came to the United States in 1979 to study engineering at the University of Alabama in Tuscaloosa. By the time he had graduated from college in 1983, Israeli reprisals against Palestinian guerrillas, who used bases in Lebanon to launch attacks against Israel, had destroyed much of southern Lebanon. When Ibrahim returned home that year, he was hopeful that peace would come soon and he would find plenty of work reconstructing sewer systems, water lines, buildings, and roads. After a year of unsuccessfully trying to make a living in Lebanon, he returned to the United States to attend graduate school.

In 1987, with a master's degree in civil engineering under his belt, Ibrahim went back to Lebanon again. Peace had largely returned to southern Lebanon, but war had destroyed the economy. Low wages and high inflation made life there very difficult. After a year, Ibrahim returned to the United States once again and found work as a highway engineer in Illinois.

Ibrahim is typical of Lebanese immigrants who came over in the second wave — mostly Muslim, highly educated people who came to the United States to escape the turmoil of war and to take advantage of opportunities here for educational and professional advancement. Like immigrants of the first wave, they, too, were looking for a better life than they had in Lebanon. And like many of the early immigrants, their love for their homeland and their hopes to return to it someday remained strong.

Second-Wave Immigrants' Ethnic Revival

In contrast to second- and third-generation Lebanese Americans, who had become very assimilated into American society, these new immigrants brought with them a keen interest in maintaining their cultural heritage. The experiences they brought with them of civil war and foreign invasion spurred the Lebanese American community here to become more politically involved in influencing U.S. foreign policy toward Lebanon. Their Arab nationalism was contagious.

The arrival of these immigrants coincided with an effort by many Lebanese Americans to revive their culture, strengthening it with their own use of Arabic and interest in their heritage. The first and most important place to nurture pride in their heritage was in the home.

A Lebanese American girl dances at a Valentine's Day party at St. Nicholas Antiochan Orthodox Cathedral in Brooklyn. The social life of most Lebanese Americans centers on their families and their churches or mosques.

CHAPTER THREE

FAMILY AND COMMUNITY
THE TIES THAT BIND

A frequently quoted Arab proverb states, "I and my brothers against my cousin; I and my cousins against the stranger." This is the traditional order of Lebanese Americans' loyalties. Obligations to one's parents, children, and siblings come first. Beyond the immediate family, allegiances extend to close relatives, then to distant ones. Lebanese Americans demonstrate this sense of loyalty to family by fulfilling their family roles, providing each other with support, and guarding the family honor.

Traditional Family Roles

Just as the lines of loyalty among Lebanese Americans are clear, so are the family roles. The important family unit for traditional Lebanese Americans is the patriarchal line: an elder man, his wife, sons, unmarried daughters, and his sons' wives. Daughters leave the family when they marry into another family.

Fathers. The father is recognized as the head of the household. His status in the extended family depends on seniority. With age comes respect.

As head of the immediate family, the father has the last word when decisions are made. But before he makes a decision, plenty of discussion and negotiation take place. Women, as well as men, voice their opinions. But when a compromise cannot be reached, the father has the final say. Whatever he decides, everyone in the family is expected to support him. Lebanese Americans consider it important for the family to put forward a unified front. Publicly criticizing the father or his opinion is seen almost as betrayal.

Mothers. In the most traditional Lebanese American families, women marry at a young age and devote their lives to caring for their homes and families. In conservative families (both Christian and Muslim), women marry young in order to ensure their virginity at the time of their weddings. The family's honor depends on it. Men, on the other hand, have to be old enough to support a wife before they can marry. Consequently, it is not unusual for women to be ten or more years younger than their husbands.

Lebanese Americans consider a woman's role of mother as the most important. She is responsible for the daily care of her children. In traditional families, mothers usually make most of the decisions directly affecting their children, such as choosing a school or a spouse for them. Although any decision is subject to approval from the father, a mother usually assumes authority over issues regarding her children.

As mistress of the house, a woman is responsible for the management of her household. She supervises the children, especially daughters, in housekeeping chores. As the household's chief hostess, she oversees the preparation of meals, the serving of coffee and tea, and the other aspects of hospitality the family shows its guests.

Even when women work outside the home, they do not usually abandon their tra-

A Lebanese American man proudly holds his grandson at a party. Generations of Lebanese Americans typically socialize together, rather than segregating themselves from one another by age, as some Americans do.

ditional roles. Many of them view their work in the home to be their primary responsibility. Work outside the home is traditionally considered secondary.

Children. Children in traditional Lebanese American families act more like adults than other American children. That is because they learn social graces from an early age. Children, even young ones, participate in all family activities. Invitations to dinners or parties are understood to include the whole family. Children attend weddings, funerals, and religious celebrations. Many traditional Lebanese Americans would not consider getting a babysitter to stay with their children while they go out. Consequently, Lebanese American children have a lot of contact with relatives and family friends of all ages.

One of the most important lessons of childhood, therefore, is learning to be polite. A child's behavior is expected to reflect well on the family. For example, children are responsible for welcoming guests to the home, just like their parents. They are taught to shake hands, exchange greetings with adults and other children, and to serve guests. Lebanese American children are expected to be able to observe table manners and polite conversation from an early age.

They are also traditionally expected to give their parents unquestioning obedience. Lebanese Americans believe children are obligated to obey their parents out of respect. If they do not, Lebanese American parents, like other parents, punish them. They typically shame their children about bad behavior. They usually point out that by misbehaving, the disobedient child is disgracing the family. Also, as in other American families, some parents spank disobedient children, whereas others deprive them of privileges.

Children's Responsibilities

Unlike other American parents who aim to teach their children to be independent, Lebanese Americans place their emphasis on being mutually supportive. Children are taught not only to take care of themselves but also to take care of each other.

That means children are expected to share the family's responsibilities, sometimes even financial ones. Everyone in the family has chores to carry out. Daughters usually help their mothers in the home. If the family owns its own business, which is typical of Lebanese Americans, young men often help their fathers at work.

Most Lebanese American parents do not encourage their children to move out of the family home when they become adults. Traditionally, daughters should stay with their parents until they marry. Sons are also likely to stay with their parents until they marry. However, that has changed to some extent because many daughters and sons now go away to college. Still, Lebanese Americans do not consider adult sons or daughters lazy for living with their parents. That is because, in a Lebanese American family, everyone helps carry the load.

Family Honor

One of the most important responsibilities of children and adults alike is to protect the family honor. Children are taught to be careful to avoid even the appearance of doing something wrong because it could hurt the family's reputation. One family member could ruin the reputation of the whole clan.

Lebanese American girls participate in Friday-night activities at Our Lady of Lebanon, a Maronite church in Brooklyn. The church provides opportunities for Lebanese Americans to gather, eat, play games, and listen to music.

The fear of bringing shame and dishonor to the family name may even be strong enough to have discouraged most Lebanese and other Arab Americans from committing crimes or accepting financial assistance from the government. According to some historians, few Arab names appear on criminal-court dockets or relief rolls, even during the difficult days of Great Depression in the 1930s.

Marriage: Making New Ties

In order to protect the families' honor, the ties made through marriage are often given great consideration not only by the couple, but also by everyone in the bride's and groom's families. The old adage "You can't choose your relatives" is not true when it comes to marriage. Among traditional Lebanese Americans, marriage is a strategically planned union of families. Like business corporations, families seek mergers that will enhance their social and economic position. The bride's family wants to guarantee her happiness, financial security, and well being. The groom's family wants to bring a daughter-in-law into the family who will reflect well on him. This approach to marriage seems very unromantic to other Americans, but many Lebanese Americans believe that the decision to marry is too important to make solely on the basis of emotion.

Another reason the choice of a spouse is considered so carefully is that for some Lebanese Americans, divorce is not an option. Some Lebanese Christians belong to churches that do not allow divorce. Muslims may divorce, but there is usually strong pressure from the family to avoid it.

A Traditional Way

In some cases, parents are very involved in helping their children find spouses. This is especially true in families of first-generation Lebanese Americans, in which the parents or even the children were born in Lebanon. When Aida Chamander entered middle school in Toledo, for example, her parents decided it was time for her to marry. They took their thirteen-year-old daughter to Lebanon so she could meet her brother-in-law's brother, Osman, who was twenty-four, to see if she liked him. Although the final decision to marry would be left up to Osman and Aida, their parents had already met and agreed that they supported the union. As it turned out, the couple liked each other, so they became engaged.

To be engaged meant the couple could visit together in Aida's home without a chaperon present, although her family was in the next room. Her parents did not consider dating proper. To go outside the home on a date as a couple could damage Aida's reputation. Many Arabs believe that if one has dated, one has been sexually active. An Arab proverb says, "Do not trust a man and a woman alone together any longer than it takes for water to run out of a jar."

Aida and Osman's engagement also meant their families could begin negotiating the marriage contract. The groom's family pledges the bride a certain amount of financial support in case he dies or the couple divorces. His family also agrees to the amount of gold jewelry it will buy for her. The jewelry would be hers to keep no matter what the future held for the couple, as a sort of insurance policy for her future. (There is no dowry from the bride's family in Arab tradition.)

Osman came to visit regularly during the two months Aida was in Lebanon. She served him coffee or tea, and the two talked together about their hopes for the future. She returned to Toledo and shared the news of her engagement with relatives and friends there.

The next year, Aida went back to Lebanon and married Osman. The couple considered staying in Lebanon, but eventually decided to leave because of the civil war. In 1982, three years after their wedding, Aida, Osman, and their two children, aided by U.S. Marines, escaped from Lebanon with a group of U.S. citizens.

Different Positions on Dating

Aida's family arranged her early marriage because, like many Muslim Lebanese Americans, they did not want their daughter to date when she became a teenager. Now a mother of five children herself, Aida says she does not want her daughters to marry as young as she did. "I thank God I have a good husband and children, but I didn't get to study the way I would have liked," she says. "I want my kids to have dreams, to do something before they get married and are tied down with the responsibilities of a family."

Aida agrees with her parents, however, that dating is not a good way to find a spouse. She does not plan to allow her own children to date. Like many other Muslims, she encourages her children to socialize with relatives and family friends instead. By doing so, she believes her children will be protected from teenage drinking, premarital sex, and drug use, all of which understandably scare most Lebanese American parents, Christians, Muslims, and Druze alike.

Aida's marriage represents a more traditional one, and even among traditional families today, it is unusual for Lebanese American women to marry at such a young age. Ali Jamal-Eddine, a Muslim Lebanese American in Cincinnati, had a typical American wedding. He married Mary Swan, an American woman he met while he was in graduate school, after the couple had dated for more than a year.

A Lebanese American teenager dances at a party. Many Lebanese American teenagers go out with groups of friends, rather than dating in boy-girl pairs.

They were married in a civil ceremony and had a reception with friends and family in a hall they rented for the occasion.

Like Ali, Ghassan Korban, a Lebanese American Christian in Milwaukee, met his wife, Laura Merola, in college and dated her before they married. But like Aida, Ghassan plans to encourage his children to go out with groups of friends rather than in pairs as other American teenagers usually do. Unlike Aida, he plans to encourage them to socialize with friends from school as well as relatives and family friends. "I want to take a middle approach," he says, "somewhere between the freedom many American kids have and the strict supervision of some Lebanese American families. I believe in teaching them my values and trusting them. I can't watch my children all the time."

As these examples show, the influence of American life has changed most Lebanese Americans' approach to courtship. The opportunities for education for both young women and men has led many Lebanese Americans to postpone marriage until finishing high school or college. Likewise, for some Lebanese Americans, school (instead of family) serves as a center of their social life, as it does for many other American teenagers. Like Aida's, Ali's, and Ghassan's families, each Lebanese American family finds its own way between their Lebanese traditions and the customs of mainstream America.

Families in Transition

American life has changed traditional Lebanese American families in other ways as well. Even decades ago, financial needs made many first-generation wives equal breadwinners with their husbands, making their work outside the home more important. Also, because a father's work sometimes kept him away for weeks or months at a time, particularly in the case of peddling, much of the decision-making for the household was done by the mother. However, most of the women felt as if they were deputies acting in the absence of the fathers, rather than actual heads of the household.

As a result of women's expanding role, the size and lifestyle of Lebanese American families changed. Although wives and mothers did not abandon their traditional roles, they found ways to lighten their work loads. First, they had fewer children. They also made less elaborate meals. And they began to adopt the American custom of prearranged social visits in place of maintaining a constant open house.

Likewise, opportunities for education have lightened the family responsibilities of children. In second- and third-generation Lebanese American families, the main job of children

WHAT'S IN A NAME?

When Lebanese Americans are introduced, they can learn a lot from each other's names. First, they discover if the person they are meeting is Christian or Muslim. Christians and Muslims usually use different names. For example, Christians are often named after Jesus' disciples or after saints. Names like George and Joseph are popular.

Muslims often use names that describe God or depict our relationship with God. For example, the male name Abd al-Aziz means "servant of the Mighty" ("Mighty" being one of the names for God). Some Muslim names, like Ahmad or Hamid, are derived from Mohammed, the prophet of Islam. Muslims also name their children after great Muslims of the past. For example, a girl might be named Aisha after the wife of the prophet, who was known as a faithful Muslim. The boy's name Ali was the name of the prophet Mohammed's cousin, one of the first to believe his message.

A Lebanese American's family name may also reveal where in Lebanon from which the family came. Villages were established by extended families that sometimes lived there for hundreds of years. Consequently, the locations of such families are widely known.

has been to study. Homework has replaced family chores as a child's chief task. Children are still expected to help in the home and, sometimes, in family businesses, but to a much lesser extent than the children of the early immigrants.

Relationships within extended families have also changed. Although Lebanese American families are still very close-knit, the ties between them have loosened in the United States. Work opportunities that spread relatives out all across the country have prevented extended families from participating in each other's lives to the degree they once did. Although affection and concern for relatives remains strong, fewer extended Lebanese American families live and work together.

Consequently, the influence of the patriarch, the eldest man in the extended family, has diminished. As newlyweds established their own households, rather than moving into the husband's father's house, the nuclear family replaced the extended family as the important family unit. Although the respect for the patriarch remains, in most families, his approval is no longer needed for decisions affecting his son's and grandson's families.

Despite the influence of American life, Lebanese Americans continue to honor their responsibilities to their families. Relationships within families are usually warm and caring. Brothers and sisters, as well as parents and children, support each other generously. For example, when Ghassan Korban's younger brother Joseph went to college, Ghassan helped

pay his way. As the first immigrant in his family, he also bought a house for his parents when they moved here. Most Lebanese Americans in the same situation as Ghassan would have done the same thing. It is not unusual for an uncle to finance a nephew's business venture, or for cousins to pool their money and become business partners. That is because, traditionally, they view their resources as their family's, rather than their own individually.

The Lebanese American Community

The support networks that were lost when extended families scattered have been recreated in community organizations. Lebanese Americans are said to love to organize. The first organizations were established along religious lines, which, in the early days, were never crossed. Even Christians of different denominations did not mix.

These first Lebanese American associations served as substitutes for churches until churches could be built. Because the first group of immigrants did not include clergy, the early

Two Lebanese American women carry a birthday cake. In Lebanese American families, women are usually responsible for hospitality and family celebrations.

immigrants organized themselves to worship, bury the dead, and help the needy. They raised money for churches and mosques and, eventually, hired clergy that came from Lebanon. As churches began to be established in the 1920s and mosques in the 1940s, they gradually took over the role of those organizations. For example, the Phoenician Club in Birmingham, Alabama, was created around 1900 as a burial society by the earliest, male settlers. When, in the 1920s, two Lebanese churches — Saint Elias Maronite Catholic Church and Saint George Melkite Greek Catholic Church — were established, the churches took the responsibility for burials. So the Phoenician Club evolved into a welcoming center for new immigrants. Today, it continues to meet as a social club, but it has changed its name to the Cedars Club.

In areas like New York, where in the early 1900s there were relatively large Lebanese American communities, other societies and clubs formed and served a variety of purposes. Some were charitable. Others helped new immigrants learn English and master the ways of their new home. Some societies encouraged patriotism and naturalization.

Social organizations, called Syrian-Lebanese Associations, developed in every state. The chief purpose of these groups has been to unite the Syrian-Lebanese American community. The individual groups participate in regional conventions that bring together Lebanese Americans for huge celebrations. Since the Lebanese assimilated so well into mainstream American life, some families have looked to these organizations as a way of helping their children maintain their Lebanese heritage.

Two Lebanese American men wait on a customer at a Lebanese deli. Shops that sell Lebanese foods and spices make it possible for Lebanese Americans to cook traditional foods in their homes.

THE LEBANESE AMERICAN PRESS

The Lebanese American press, which was very active until the end of World War II, helped immigrants adjust to American life while, at the same time, encouraging them to preserve their ethnic heritage.

The first Lebanese American newspaper was published in New York in 1892. The newspaper, called *Kawkah Amrika* ("The Star of America"), brought the Lebanese and Syrian community news from the homeland and Syrian folklore in Arabic.

Another early paper that was particularly influential was the Maronites' *Al-Hoda* ("The Guidance"), started in 1898. About the same time, the Eastern Orthodox and the Druze also began their own publications, called *Mirat al-Gharb* ("Mirror of the West") and *al-Bayan* ("The Explanation"), respectively. These publications, all in Arabic, informed immigrants of customs, policies, laws, and manners they would need to know in the United States. They also fostered the bonds between immigrants and Lebanon by providing news of happenings in their native land.

In the 1920s, when first-generation Lebanese Americans were adapting so well to American life that some in the community feared they would lose their own cultural heritage, newspapers and magazines began appearing that aimed to foster ethnic pride. Those newspapers were published in English because, by then, many Lebanese Americans did not speak Arabic.

The most significant of these publications was *Syrian World,* first published in 1926. It served as a forum for the Lebanese and Syrian American community, influencing public opinion within the community and rallying support for causes affecting it. One writer whose opinions appeared in *Syrian World* was Kahlil Gibran, the famous poet, painter, and essayist whose book *The Prophet* is still a best seller today. The magazine folded in 1932, during the Great Depression.

Since then, Lebanese American publications have not spoken to a national audience. Most publications today exist for the benefit of local communities or particular organizations.

One underlying purpose of the social organizations has been to provide Lebanese American youth with a chance to meet other Lebanese Americans. David Herro, president of the Syrian-Lebanese Midwest Federation Young Adult Network, says his organization is "practically a dating service." His mother, Debbie, says parents feel comfortable with relationships established through the Federation. Through conventions, meetings, parties, and the like, the families that participate tend to know each other well. For the Herro family, the conventions are a family reunion because relatives from many states regularly attend.

Families rather than individuals usually join the Lebanese American social organizations, thus demonstrating how family oriented Lebanese Americans are. Whereas other Americans may think of themselves primarily as individuals, Lebanese Americans continue to see themselves as extensions of their families. They worship and socialize together as families rather than as individuals. Their personal decisions are usually made through family discussions. No matter how Americanized they become, Lebanese Americans still honor their traditional loyalty to family first.

Two Muslim men talk with the imam (an Islamic cleric) at the Islamic Cultural Center of New York. Muslims often seek advice from imams about how to apply the teachings of the Koran, the holy book of Islam.

CHAPTER FOUR

RELIGION AND CELEBRATIONS
FAITH OF THEIR FATHERS

When seventeen-year-old Said Audi moved to the United States from Lebanon in 1985, one of the first things he did was find an Eastern Orthodox church to attend. He grew up in Kasrhazir, Lebanon, a town located in a region where 90 to 95 percent of Lebanon's Eastern Orthodox Christians live. His church there had played a central role in his childhood.

When his mother came to the United States in 1994 to see Said get his doctoral degree in biomedical engineering, he took her to St. George Orthodox Church of Boston in the suburb of West Roxbury. The Boston church felt very familiar to her. Although it was less than 'one hundred years old, everything about its worship service, except the use of English, mirrored the services of her ancient church in Kasrhazir.

During the regular Sunday service, Said watched the altar boys. "I could predict every move they were going to make," he says. Said was an altar boy in Kasrhazir from the time he was nine until he was fourteen. He had worn a white robe and carried a heavy metal cross in front of the priest in a procession, just as the altar boys in Boston did.

When the altar boys disappeared from his view at the altar in front of the church in

Altar boys assist with the sacrament of communion at St. Nicholas Antiochan Orthodox Cathedral in Brooklyn.

Boston, Said knew that some were cutting the heavy, leavened bread for the Holy Communion. Another might be lighting incense. Later, when an altar boy held a candle on a stick above the head of a young man who read from the Bible, "to symbolize the illumination we get from the scriptures," Said remembered that he had done that himself about fifteen years ago. This same ritual has been performed the same way by altar boys for hundreds of years.

The traditional Eastern Orthodox service that Father Christopher Holwey leads at St. George Orthodox Church of Boston every Sunday feeds the senses, the priest says. The congregation "sees the beauty of the kingdom of heaven through the icons. They smell the sweetness of God's presence in the incense. They taste the body and the blood of Christ in the communion. The church is here to awaken our senses to God."

When the Eastern Orthodox liturgy, the prescribed form of the religious service, was created more than sixteen hundred years ago, most people were uneducated, explains Said. The worship service taught them about their faith through stories, dramatizations, and symbolism. By using this same ancient liturgy, Eastern Orthodox Christians in the United States have been able to preserve their religious heritage.

Of the three main Lebanese Christian denominations (the Maronite, the Melkite, and the Eastern Orthodox), the Eastern Orthodox have been the most vigilant about keeping their traditions. The worship service in Boston that Said attended was almost identical to any Eastern Orthodox service conducted in Lebanon or anywhere else in the world.

Yet American life has had an impact on all three Lebanese Christian groups. To understand what the Eastern Orthodox, the Melkites, and the Maronites have become in the United States, we must first understand who they were in Lebanon.

Lebanese American Christians

Most of the Lebanese immigrants who came to the United States in the early 1900s were Christians. Even though the majority of people in the United States were also Christians, many of the Lebanese Christians found they did not fit into either of America's major Christian categories: Protestant or Catholic. Although they were Catholics, they brought with them brands of the faith that differed in important ways from America's Roman Catholic Church. Those differences resulted from their separate histories.

The Melkites and the Eastern Orthodox

Many of the early Lebanese immigrants to the United States were Melkite and Eastern Orthodox. After the great schism of 1054, when the Catholic Church divided into the Byzantine and Roman churches, both the Melkites and the Eastern Orthodox evolved under the Byzantine tradition. But the French sent missionaries to convert the Byzantines to the Roman Catholic Church. Consequently, in 1724, a group of Byzantines associated with the Roman Catholic Church and became known as Melkites. The Melkite Church kept its Eastern traditions, however, and remained more similar in its practices to the Eastern Orthodox Church, from which it came, than to the Roman Catholic Church.

Both the Eastern Orthodox and the Melkites are proud of their long histories. They trace their churches back to the first Christian church in Antioch, established by Jesus' disciple Peter. The liturgy (ritual), which is still used in both denominations, was created in the fourth century. The sacraments (rituals begun by Jesus) of baptism, Chrismation (confirmation), and the Eucharist (communion) have been conducted in the same way for hundreds of years. However, the Lebanese Christians found that most Americans are unaware of the existence of the Eastern churches and know nothing of their distinguished history. Consequently, both Eastern Orthodox and Melkite Christians found that, in the United States, they have often had to defend their faiths.

Maronites

The third important group of Lebanese American Christians are the Maronites. They also trace their roots back to Antioch. The Maronite church began in the fifth century A.D. when a group of Christians, following a monk named Maron, separated from the ancient Syriac church. They believed the Syriac church was moving away from the true Catholic faith.

From the beginning, the Maronites have been faithful to Rome. They were never part of the Byzantine Church. However, the early Maronites developed their own liturgy in the ancient Syriac language. The Syriac liturgy is still used today, but it is supplemented with English and Arabic. Consequently, their liturgy is unique — different from the one used by the Melkites and the Eastern Orthodox and also different from the Roman Catholic liturgy.

When Muslims from the Arabian peninsula came to Lebanon in the eighth century, spreading the Islamic faith, sometimes by force, the Maronites sought refuge in the mountains of Lebanon. They were led from Syria to Lebanon by their first patriarch, St. John Maron, and built their first church in Lebanon in the year 749.

Because of their loyalty to the Roman Catholic Church, the Maronites in Lebanon developed close ties with the West, particularly with France, which sent Crusaders and missionaries to Lebanon. Consequently, the Maronites became very westernized in both theology and culture. Such expressions of Western devotional life as the rosary and the stations of the cross were introduced into the Maronite Church. Their Western views caused distance, and sometimes resentment and fighting, between the Maronites and other Lebanese Christians.

When Lebanese Christians immigrated to the United States, they brought their separate religious loyalties with them. Consequently, the early Lebanese American community was not a unified one. It was divided along religious lines. And each religious group's experience in the United States was distinct.

Lebanese Christian Places of Worship

In America, the early Lebanese immigrants preceded their churches. Before a church could be established, there had to be a community of believers to support it. Therefore, some Lebanese Christians joined existing American churches. The Melkites and the Maronites tended to affiliate with Roman Catholic churches, and the Eastern Orthodox joined with Episcopal churches, whose religious traditions reminded them of their own. Some Eastern Orthodox also attended Russian or Greek Orthodox masses.

However, those who joined existing American churches never really felt they belonged. They were looked upon as foreigners who had converted. Their own religious traditions were unknown or considered backward by other American Catholics.

In communities where there were no Eastern churches, those who remained faithful to their own traditions met together in homes or club halls to worship. Melkites in one city visited the home of an immigrant who displayed an icon (a symbolic painting) of St. George in her living room. They came to pray and light candles before it. The woman had brought the icon from her tiny church in Lebanon, which had been demolished to make way for a new church building. When the prayers of that local Lebanese American community were answered, they would send donations to the church in Lebanon.

Traveling priests made sporadic visits to communities where there were no churches. The Lebanese Christians in those communities waited for the priests to perform important ceremonies like weddings and baptisms.

Melkites and Maronites Under Pressure to Conform

The Melkites and Maronites, because their churches had united with the Roman Catholic Church, found themselves under considerable pressure to conform to the ways of American Roman Catholics. In order to protect their Eastern traditions, both groups had requested to be allowed to establish their own independent dioceses, but Rome did not respond. Until the 1960s, the Roman Catholic Church held the position that it would be better for those groups to be integrated into the American Catholic Church. Consequently, for a time, the Melkite and Maronite churches lost much of their Eastern flavor.

By 1966, the Melkites and Maronites were finally allowed to have their own bishops. They were also encouraged by the Roman Catholic Church's new position that the Eastern churches should return to their old traditions. Then a campaign began to reclaim their religious heritage.

Melkite churches around the country restored the Church's Eastern tradition by removing all the distinctly Roman symbols,

like the statues of saints, the holy water fonts, the altar rail, the confessional booth, and the stations of the cross. Latin-style altars were taken down and replaced with Byzantine Holy Tables. The use of rosaries for prayer was dropped. Choirs were taught to chant the Byzantine liturgy.

Icons — pictures of Jesus and the saints that were not realistic portraits but were intended to show lives changed by God — replaced Roman Catholic statues. As one Melkite priest put it, "Icons serve as windows that allow us to see into heaven." The Melkite and Eastern Orthodox Christians preferred icons to statues because they associate statues with the Greek and Roman pagans, who created statues of their gods.

In contrast to the Melkites, the Maronites kept many of the Latin traditions, such as the use of rosaries and stations of the cross, because they had adopted them long ago and felt those practices were now part of their own tradition. However, in the 1970s, the Maronites did restore their Sunday liturgy to its origins by returning to the Maronite yearly cycle of prayers and hymns. They also replaced Roman prayers at certain places in the service with traditional Maronite prayers and incense.

Eastern Orthodox Christians

Unlike the Maronites and Melkites, the Eastern Orthodox were not under great pressure to conform because they had not joined the Roman Catholic Church. On the other hand, they were always having to explain themselves to Americans who had never heard of them.

But even the Orthodox churches could not escape from U.S. influence. Over time, fewer members of the religious community could speak Arabic, so in many churches, English came to replace Arabic as the liturgical lan-

The priest leads the service at St. Nicholas Antiochan Orthodox Cathedral in Brooklyn. The Eastern Orthodox service is noted for its dramatic pageantry.

guage. In some churches, cantors, soloists who sang the liturgy, were phased out in favor of choirs, and the liturgy was shortened.

Eastern Orthodox and Melkite Traditions and Celebrations

In spite of the changes made in church services in the United States, the Eastern Orthodox and Melkite churches retained many of their traditions. Holy Communion is observed every Sunday. The leavened bread for the Eucharist is baked in a flat, round loaf called *Kurban* and is stamped with a seal that impresses the sign of the cross and Greek letters symbolizing Christ in the dough. Families wishing to have a deceased loved one remembered bake the Kurban for the service. The priest takes communion himself, then the sacraments are shared with parishioners. Following the liturgical prayers, the remaining portions of the Kurban are distributed and eaten.

Children, even those under seven (the age of reason in the Roman Catholic Church), take communion in the Eastern Orthodox and Melkite churches. The reason those churches allow even infants to take communion is that they say communion feeds children spiritually. The reasoning is that just as one would not starve a child physically until the age of seven by withholding food, one should not starve the child spiritually by withholding spiritual nourishment.

Likewise, children play an active role in the celebration of holidays. In the Eastern Orthodox and Melkite churches, ceremonies marking religious holidays require participation. Everyone takes part in the ceremony.

Easter. Easter (or *Pascha,* which means "Passover," as it is called in the Eastern Orthodox Church) is the Church's most important holiday. A midnight service is held that dramatizes the victory of Christ over Satan.

An icon, or symbolic painting, of the Virgin Mary and Jesus. In Eastern Orthodox and Melkite churches, icons serve as "windows to the kingdom of God" by showing lives that are changed by Christ.

The service begins with the priest standing in a dark church, holding a burning candle in front of the congregation, and saying, "Come, take light from the light that is never overcome by night." Members of the congregation come forward and light their candles from his.

Then, the congregation gathers outside the church, each member holding a lighted candle. One person stays in the dark church, playing the part of Satan. The priest, representing Christ, bangs loudly on the church door and cries, "Open the doors so the King of Glory can enter." Satan answers, "Who is the King of Glory?" The priest answers, "The Lord, strong and mighty; the Lord, mighty in battle." The dialogue is repeated three times; then the priest throws open the doors, Satan runs out, and the lights in the church go on. Then the congregation sings, *"Al Maseeh Kam"* ("Christ is risen.")

After the service, the Lenten fast is broken by eating an Easter egg. In Lebanon, children gather vegetable roots and onion and pomegranate skins to make red dyes for the eggs. In the United States, those natural dyes have been replaced with store-bought ones. The eggs are dyed red, symbolizing the blood of Christ, and are taken to the priest to be blessed. The Easter eggs are distributed to the congregation after the service. Everyone greets each other and hits the eggs together to symbolize the breaking open of Christ's tomb.

Epiphany. Epiphany is another important celebration for the Eastern Orthodox and Melkite churches. It is celebrated on the twelfth day after Christmas to commemorate the baptism of Jesus in the Jordan River, when, Christians say, God's voice was heard declaring, "This is my beloved Son, with whom I am well pleased." Special Epiphany services are held in the church. Also, during the week of Epiphany, priests visit the homes of their parishioners and bless corners of the rooms with holy water. Families serve *zalabee,* a fried doughnut cake, to the priest and other visitors during the week of Epiphany. The sweet cake symbolizes the sweetness of the new spiritual life that begins at baptism.

Maronite Holidays

The Maronites had adopted many of the traditions of the Roman Catholic Church long before they came to the United States. Those traditions have been a part of Maronite practice for so long that Maronites consider them their own. Consequently, the sacraments of baptism, confirmation, and communion in the Maronite Church are identical to the Roman Catholic practices. Likewise, Maronites celebrate Easter, Christmas, the Epiphany, and other Christian holidays as Roman Catholics do.

Maronites also continue to celebrate two holidays that originated with the Maronite Church. On February 9, the Church observes St. Maron Day, a day of tribute to the Maronites' patron saint that features a special liturgy.

Maronites also honor their first patriarch, St. John Maron, on March 2. This occasion is also marked with its own liturgy.

Lebanese American Muslims

In contrast to the early Lebanese Christian immigrants, Lebanese Muslims who immigrated before World War II did not find congregations they could join. Many Muslims were afraid to come to a country where they would be far outnumbered by Christians, a country of "unbelievers," where there were no mosques, people worked on Friday, and no calls to prayer were heard during the day. But the need to support their families and escape Turkish oppression finally brought Muslims to the States.

About 10 percent of the Lebanese immigrants who came before World War II were Muslims. Because of their reluctance to come to a largely Christian country, those who came followed the Christian Lebanese immigrants by about twenty years, with most arriving between 1915 and 1921.

Bringing a New Faith to a New Land

Despite the immigrants' fears, Islam proved to be very portable because it is a personal faith that can be practiced by individuals without clergy or sacraments. A single Muslim could practice his or her faith even when he or she was the only Muslim in town.

Still, in the early days, Muslims missed the support of a religious community. As the number of Muslims in the United States gradually increased, communal prayer services were held, and, eventually, mosques were built. The first mosque in the United States was built in Highland Park, Michigan (near Detroit), in 1919. The second mosque was built in Michigan City, Indiana, in 1924. The third mosque in the nation was founded in 1929 in Ross, North Dakota, by a community of Lebanese immigrants who peddled wares to local farmers. Most of the other mosques that exist in the United Sates today were built after World War II.

The second major wave of Lebanese immigrants, who came between 1967 and 1985, included more Muslims than Christians. These Muslims came to a country that had mosques established by the early Muslim immigrants. When these Lebanese arrived, they found many opportunities for worship and fellowship with other Muslims.

That is because Islam, through birth, immigration, and conversion, is the fastest growing religion in the United States today.

There are presently about four to five million Muslims in the United States (exact numbers are not available because the U.S. Census does not ask people to identify their religion), making Islam larger than several mainline Protestant denominations, such as the Presbyterians, Episcopalians, and Assemblies of God. Scholars generally agree that by the year 2000, Islam will become the nation's second-largest religion. (It is already the second-largest religion in the world, following Christianity.)

Another indication of the growth of Islam in the United States is the increase in the number of mosques. Since 1986, the number of mosques and Islamic student centers grew from 598 to more than 1,100, with at least one in every state.

Islam's growth in the United States has caused religious leaders here to change the way they refer to the common beliefs and values many Americans share. What they formerly called the "Judeo-Christian" heritage, some are calling "Abrahamic," a term that traces the common spiritual roots of Christians, Jews, and Muslims to Abraham, the patriarch of all three faiths. With the change in terminology, U.S. religious leaders are recognizing that Islam is no longer a foreign faith.

Being Muslim in the United States

When eighteen-year-old Mohamad el-Kassem came to the United States from Lebanon in 1980, he took his Islamic faith for granted. He was a Muslim in name, but he did not practice his faith. He rarely did any of the five daily prayers that are required of all Muslims, nor did he regularly fast from sunrise to sunset during the holy month of Ramadan.

"Here in America, I learned to practice real Islam," says Mohamad. As a university student, he met other Muslims from the Middle East who gathered for fellowship. He saw the contrast between the faithful Muslims who never drank alcohol and other college students who often got drunk on the weekends. "When you live in a society that is not Islamic, you see why you need to be a Muslim," he says.

Now a civil engineer in Los Angeles, Mohamad enjoys the support of an active Islamic community. His wife, Hala, and their children, six-year-old Zeina and four-year-old Monzer, attend the Islamic Center downtown, one of greater Los Angeles' fifty-four mosques. His children learn about Islam in a Sunday school class offered at the mosque. Every year on the Eid al-Fitr, the feast day following Ramadan (the holy month of fasting), the family joins close to fifteen thousand people who meet in the downtown convention center for a special prayer service. Then they usually go on a picnic with friends, enjoying the holiday outside as many Muslims in Lebanon do.

In the United States, Mohamad and his family join Muslims from a wide variety of ethnic backgrounds in worship and fellowship. His children have an opportunity to see that there are people of all races and backgrounds who embrace Islam, that it is not just the religion of the Arabs.

Although there are many opportunities in Los Angeles for fellowship with other Muslims, Mohamad thinks that living in the United States presents some challenges in raising Muslim children. In his daughter's public school, for example, Christmas, Hanukkah, and Valentine's Day are observed, but the Muslim Eid is not. Mohamad objects to his children learning Christmas carols and being expected to bring cards to classmates on Valentine's Day, a holiday honoring a Christian saint.

Another problem many Muslims say they have here is that many non-Muslim Americans don't know much about Islam. And, often, what they think they know is wrong, Muslims

Muslims at the Islamic Cultural Center of New York discuss their beliefs with the imam, an Islamic cleric.

say. For example, Muslims say that the phrase "Islamic fundamentalists" that appears frequently in the U.S. media, describing someone who has committed an act of terrorism, gives the false impression that Islam condones violence against innocent people. Also, the role of Muslim women is often misunderstood by non-Muslim Americans, Muslims say. They point out that many stereotypes, such as that of the Muslim woman who is limited to housework and child care and not allowed to contribute to the larger society through a career or other activities, have no basis in the Koran, the holy book of Islam.

In spite of the difficulties that sometimes arise from living in a country where the majority of people are Christians, Mohamad believes Muslim Americans should not separate themselves from the greater community but should actively participate in it. Muslim Americans have a responsibility to be a good influence on this country, he says. He hopes to do that by practicing his Islamic faith.

Islamic Beliefs and Practices

The meaning of the word *Islam* is "submission" or "peace." A Muslim is one who submits to God. To become a Muslim, one must declare and believe that "There is no deity except God and Mohammed is his prophet." This confession of faith is called the *shahadah,* "the witness," and has been declared by Muslims since Mohammed's time.

As they declare in the shahadah, Muslims believe there is one, and only one, God. The Arabic word for God is *Allah.* It is not a name of a special Islamic deity. When Muslims refer to Allah, they are referring to the one supreme being that is the same for Muslims, Christians, and Jews. In fact, Arabic-speaking Christians also address God as Allah.

Muslims believe God is all powerful, eternal, infinitely good, and merciful. They believe God harshly punishes the wicked but forgives those who sincerely ask him. They believe there is a day of judgment, an afterlife, heaven, and hell.

To assert the second half of the shahadah is to agree that the Prophet Mohammed's revelations, which are recorded in the Koran, are really coming from God. Islam traces its origin to the seventh century, when, Muslims believe, the Prophet Mohammed received divine revelations from the angel Gabriel, which were recorded in the Koran. The Koran is the prime source of a Muslim's faith and practice. The other source of guidance for Muslims

THE KORAN: THE HOLY BOOK OF ISLAM

Islam asserts that the Koran is the final link in a chain of revealed scriptures. Muslims believe it was revealed to Mohammed, the prophet of Islam, through the angel Gabriel during a twenty-three-year period between Mohammed's fortieth year and his death. It speaks of God's existence and power and of humans' relationship to God. It also declares moral principles to govern our lives, both individually and collectively.

The following translation of verses from the Koran explains Islam's position on the relationship between the Torah (the Five Books of Moses, which make up most of the Jewish Scriptures), the Christian Bible, and the Koran:

"And before this was the Scripture of Moses as a guide and a mercy. And this Scripture [the Koran] confirms it in the Arabic tongue, to warn the wrong-doers and as glad tidings to those who do good." (46:12)

"And in their footsteps We [God] sent Jesus the son of Mary. . . . We gave him the *Injeel* [the original scripture revealed to Jesus]; therein was guidance and light, and confirmation of what is in hand of the *Taurat* [the Hebrew Torah, or original scripture revealed to Moses], a guidance and an admonition to those who fear God." (5:46)

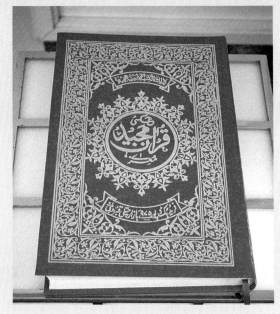

"It is He Who revealed to Thee [Mohammed] the Scripture [the Koran] in truth, confirming what is in hand of the scriptures that went before it. And He revealed the *Taurat* and the *Injeel* before this as guidance to mankind. And He revealed the Criterion [rules for judging right from wrong]. . . ." (3:3-4)

Muslims believe that the similarities between the great monotheistic religions — Judaism, Christianity, and Islam — come from a common origin, namely from God's revelations to human beings.

comes from examples from Mohammed's life and teaching that are passed down in stories called *Hadith.*

In the Muslim's view, Mohammed did not begin a new religion. The Koran contains the same truth that God revealed to all his prophets, beginning with Adam and including Abraham, Moses, and Jesus. But, according to Islamic beliefs, the revelation to Mohammed was God's final message to humankind, a reconfirmation of earlier revelations. Consequently, Muslims believe that Islam, Judaism, and Christianity have a common origin.

The Five Pillars of Islam

In Islamic beliefs, there are five acts of worship that are required of Muslims: the declaration of faith, the prescribed prayers, fasting, tithing (the *zakat),* and the pilgrimage to Mecca. Together they are called the *ibadat,* which means "pillars."

Witnessing. The first act of worship is to declare one's belief that there is only one God and that Mohammed is his prophet. When someone converts to Islam, he or she makes this declaration in the mosque in front of other Muslims. The purpose is to let other Muslims know they have a new Muslim brother or sister. Children who grow up in the Muslim faith need not make this statement before a congregation, but they are taught to say the shahadah regularly to themselves.

Prayer. The second act of worship is to perform the prescribed prayers. Muslims should pray five times a day: at dawn, noon, mid-afternoon, sunset and nightfall. In these prayers, the worshiper recites verses from the Koran in Arabic while facing Mecca, which is in Saudi Arabia. Muslims consider Mecca holy because it was where they believe Abraham built his temple, known in Arabic as the *Ka'ba.*

When praying, Muslims must stand on clean ground, without shoes. The cleanliness of the ground is often provided by the use of a prayer mat or a prayer rug. While reciting the prayers, the worshipers bow, stand upright again, then kneel and prostrate themselves, putting their foreheads to the ground, and then sit back on their heels. As they pray, Muslims give thanks to God. These ritual prayers, in which the worshiper praises and thanks God, are called *salat* and differ from other types of prayer in which one asks God for help or asks for God's blessing, which are called *du'a.* A Muslim may pray du'a whenever he or she wants and is not required to kneel and bow when praying. Du'a is not one of the required acts of faith but is often practiced by Muslims.

Fasting. The third act of worship, fasting, lasts for one month, called Ramadan. This month has special significance because it is the month in which Muslims believe the Koran was revealed to Mohammed.

Because Muslims use a different calendar from the solar-based Gregorian calendar, Ramadan occurs a little earlier each year. The Muslim calendar is a lunar calendar, divided into twelve months. Because the calendar is based on phases of the moon, months are either twenty-nine or thirty days long.

During Ramadan, Muslims fast from the first light of dawn until sundown, abstaining from food, drink, and sexual relations. In addition, they make a special effort to be patient and control their anger. There are exceptions to the fasting rule for anyone who is sick, elderly, on a journey, pregnant, or nursing. Children are not required to fast until puberty, although many start earlier.

Fasting has several purposes. First, it is an act of obedience to God. Also, by abstaining from worldly comforts, a fasting person learns to empathize with those who go hungry. Mus-

At a mosque in the Midwest, men and boys celebrate the feast day Eid al-Fitr, which marks the end of Ramadan, a month-long time during which devout Muslims fast during the days.

lims also believe that by exercising control of their physical desires, they grow spiritually.

Tithing. The fourth pillar, tithing, called *zakat,* is based on the belief that all things belong to God. Each person sets aside a portion (usually at least 2.5 percent of one's income each year) for the poor. The zakat is collected at mosques and distributed based on guidelines in the Koran. Voluntary charity in addition to tithing is also encouraged.

Pilgrimage. The fifth and final pillar or act of worship in Islam, the pilgrimage to Mecca in Saudi Arabia, is called the *Hajj.* It is obligatory to all those who are physically and financially able to go. Abraham is believed to have established the settlement there and built the Ka'ba, a sacred place of worship. American Muslims face east, toward the Ka'ba, when they pray and should try to make a pilgrimage there at least once in a lifetime. About two

million people go to Mecca each year for the Hajj. Once a man has gone on the pilgrimage, he gains the title of *Haj;* a woman is referred to as *Haji.* Both terms mean "pilgrim."

Muslim Celebrations

The two big celebrations for Muslims are both called the *Eid.* At the end of Ramadan, the *Eid al-Fitr* is held. This is a day of feasting to mark the end of the month-long fast. Muslims in the United States, where the majority of people are not Muslims, make a special effort to make the day special for the Islamic community. They come to the mosque for prayer services on the morning of the Eid. Some communities gather for potluck dinners, banquets, or picnics. Many Lebanese American parents give their children gifts for the Eid, a custom adopted from the Christmas celebration that is so prevalent in the United States. Some families also decorate their homes with colored lights. Relatives and friends give children money and candy.

Relatives usually gather for a feast of lamb and rice. Because not all Muslims can afford the holiday trimmings, Muslims make a special donation called *zakat al-fitr*. This donation is used to help needy families in the community better enjoy the holiday by buying new clothes and food for a feast. The Eid is also an occasion to restore peace and friendships. Muslims should not let the sun set on the Eid without having made peace with anyone with whom they have unreconciled differences.

The *Eid al-Adha,* the other major Muslim holiday, is a celebration of the Hajj. Members of the Muslim community who are returning from the pilgrimage to Mecca are honored with gifts, prayers, and visits. The Haj and Haji often have gifts for relatives and friends they brought back with them from Saudi Arabia.

Druze Lebanese Americans

A smaller but important religious group that emigrated from Lebanon are the Druze. The Druze faith began in the eleventh century when the sect broke away from the Shiite Muslims over the claim of a *caliph* (the political and spiritual head of an Islamic state), al Hakim, to be the incarnation of God. (The Shiites are the second-largest sect of Islam. After the death of the Prophet Mohammed, the Shiites separated from the Sunni Muslims over a disagreement about who should succeed Mohammed as the political leader of Islam.) Despite these ties to Islam, however, most Muslims and many Druze do not consider the Druze to be Muslims.

The Druze faith got its name from a tailor, Ismael Darazi, who believed al Hakim's claim that he was God incarnate. Darazi preached to people in Lebanon, bringing them the message of al Hakim. *Darazi* means "tailor," of which *Druze* is the plural form.

The Druze share one holiday with Muslims, Eid al-Adha, commemorating the Haj. They also accept many Islamic teachings but do not necessarily observe the five pillars of the Islamic faith. They also do not allow men to have more than one wife, as Muslims do.

The Druze believe there is one God, who was reincarnated on earth once for each Age of the World (seventy times in all) and finally in the person of al Hakim. Druze do not believe anyone could convert to the faith after the disappearance of al Hakim. The Druze do not believe al Hakim actually died, and they await his return as their messiah.

Druze believe that each soul is reborn in a higher existence if the person has led a good life and that it will ultimately be absorbed into the Deity. Souls of individuals who lead bad lives are reborn as camels or dogs.

The details of the faith are known only to a small, inner circle of religious elite. Not until age forty can one join that inner circle, and only 15 percent, or one in seven, Druze ever do. Those who do join the inner circle become initiated into all the secrets of the faith. Those "Knowledgeable Ones" wear white turbans to symbolize the purity of their lives. No Druze place of worship has been established in the United States because none can be established without a resident member of the religious elite to officiate — and these men are forbidden by Druze law to emigrate from Lebanon.

Still, religion plays an important role in the life of Lebanese American Druze, as it does for many Lebanese Americans, both Christians and Muslims. Religion has always been, and probably always will be, a central part of Lebanese culture, wherever Lebanese are found. Lebanese Americans have transplanted their faiths firmly in U.S. soil.

A Lebanese American boy enjoys dessert. Relaxed family dinners help keep Lebanese American families strong.

CHAPTER FIVE

CUSTOMS, EXPRESSIONS, AND HOSPITALITY
BREAKING BREAD TOGETHER

The aroma of coffee and cardamom greets fourteen-year-old Chirrinne Zaitouni of St. Petersburg, Florida, when she returns home from school. Her mother is serving Turkish coffee for her six aunts who visit frequently. Chirrinne greets each of her aunts with a handshake and kisses on each cheek.

In the evening, other relatives arrive. Chirrinne and her family meet them with the greeting *"Ahlan wa sahlan,"* meaning "Welcome." After everyone has arrived, they all gather around a table to share a meal of *tabbouleh* (a salad of parsley and cracked wheat) and a platter of lamb and rice garnished with pine nuts. They tear pieces from flat, round loaves of pita bread, called *khobaz,* and use them to scoop up *hummus,* a flavorful dip made of crushed chick peas, lemon juice, garlic, and olive oil.

After dinner, hot tea with mint is served in clear glass cups the size of shot glasses. Then Chirrinne's father lights the *arghileh,* a Turk-

TABBOULEH

Ingredients
1 cup cracked (bulgar) wheat
1 bunch green onions
2 large bunches parsley
1/2 bunch mint
4 large tomatoes
Juice of 4 lemons
1/2 cup olive oil
Salt and pepper to taste

Directions
Soak wheat in water a few minutes. Squeeze dry by pressing between palms. Chop onions, parsley, mint leaves, and tomatoes very fine. Add wheat, lemon juice, olive oil, salt and pepper. Mix well. Serve with fresh lettuce leaves, grape leaves, or cabbage leaves used as scoops. Serves 6.

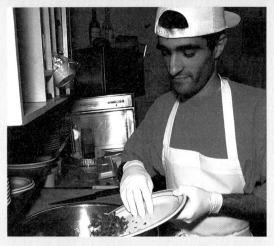

— Recipe from *The Art of Syrian Cookery: A Culinary Trip to the Land of Bible History, Syria and Lebanon,* by Helen Corey (New York: Doubleday, 1962).

Tasty Lebanese cuisine at a Middle Eastern restaurant. Counterclockwise, starting at the far left: hummus, baba ghanouj, tabbouleh, olives, pita bread, and, in the platter at the center, a salad and shish kebab on a bed of rice.

ish water pipe. As he and Chirrinne's uncles smoke, the fragrance of sweet tobacco quickly wafts through the house. The sound of the bubbling water is soon drowned out by laughter and loud discussions in Arabic.

Through moments like these, Chirrinne sees, smells, speaks, and tastes her Lebanese heritage every day. "It's in the food we eat, the way we dress, the way we talk," she says. It is in many Lebanese American families' traditions, gestures, music, dancing, and manners — in the many ways they express themselves.

Food and Fellowship

Breaking bread together with friends, neighbors, and relatives has long been a way of extending and maintaining friendships in the Lebanese tradition. Lebanese Americans carry on the tradition, frequently inviting guests to share meals with them. Some families regularly cook more than they need for themselves just in case friends drop by at supper time.

Chirrinne's uncles, aunts, and cousins often come by for dinner or invite Chirrinne and her family to their homes.

When her grandparents visit from Ohio, Chirrinne helps her mother prepare a special meal to honor their visit. Lamb is the meat of choice for special occasions. For important celebrations, like wedding dinners, a whole roasted lamb is stuffed with rice and pine nuts and served on a large silver platter. Appetizers like hummus and *baba ghanouj* (a dip made from grilled eggplant, sesame seed paste, lemon juice, and garlic), which are scooped from common dishes with pieces of pita bread, accompany the main course.

When the weather is warm, Lebanese Americans favor entertaining outside as their ancestors did in Lebanon's mild Mediterranean climate. Marinated lamb-and-vegetable *shish kebab* skewers are roasted on a grill. Ground beef or lamb mixed with parsley and onions, called *keftah,* is also grilled. Grape leaves, rolled and stuffed with rice and ground meat, are another festive favorite.

Chirrinne's mother prepares special Lebanese dishes for holidays and religious celebrations. Among the Eastern Orthodox Christians, meat dishes, such as stuffed cabbage and grape leaves, and *kibby,* made of crushed wheat and ground lamb mixed with spices, are served just prior to Lent. The boiled egg is the last food eaten before beginning the Lenten fast. Eastern Orthodox Christians eat no meat, eggs, milk, or cheese during all fast days. During the seven weeks of Lent, they eat dishes prepared without meat but with vegetables and oil. The Lenten fast is broken on Easter with the eating of the Easter egg. Fasting is also observed every Wednesday and Friday throughout the year and on other designated days.

Muslim Lebanese Americans also serve special foods during Ramadan, their month-long fast. Those observing Ramadan abstain from any eating or drinking from sunrise to sunset. Families rise in the wee hours of the morning to pray together and to share a breakfast of cheese, yogurt, olives, and pita bread. Muslims break their fast at sunset by eating dates, following the example of the Prophet Mohammed. Ramadan suppers begin with soups served especially during the holy month. Lentil soup and *kishik* are popular. Kishik is a soup made of plain yogurt, ground wheat, and spices. The yogurt is dried under the sun and crushed together with the wheat and spices into a fine powder. Lebanese Americans usually purchase the powder from Middle Eastern food markets. Evening meals during Ramadan are times for festive gatherings. Relatives and friends treat each other to feasts every evening. In some communities, worshipers gather at mosques for potluck dinners throughout the month.

HUMMUS

Ingredients:
2 (15-ounce) cans garbanzo beans (chick peas), undrained
3 small cloves garlic
1/4 cup plus 1 tablespoon tahini (sesame seed paste)
1/4 cup fresh lemon juice
3 tablespoons water

Directions:
Drain garbanzo beans, reserving 1/4 cup liquid, and set aside. Position knife blade in food processor bowl. Drop garlic through food chute with processor running and process 3 seconds or until minced. Add garbanzo beans, reserved 1/4 cup liquid, and remaining ingredients; process 3 minutes or until smooth.

Spoon mixture into a serving bowl. Serve with pita bread and raw vegetables. Yield: 3 cups (serving size: 1/4 cup).

— Recipe from Cindy Hyle Bezek, a recipe developer in Oswego, New York, published in *Cooking Light,* May 1994.

Fa-toosh, a vegetable and bread salad, is a favorite dish for both Christians and Muslims during their periods of fasting. Bite-size pieces of hard pita bread are mixed with finely chopped green onions, parsley, and cucumber tossed with olive oil, lemon juice, sumac, salt, and pepper. Likewise, lamb is served by both Christians and Muslims during the feasts that mark the ends of their periods of fasting. Muslims celebrate the *Eid al-Fitr,* a day of feasting and celebration following Ramadan. Easter marks the end of Lent.

A Lebanese American woman sells Middle Eastern spices, nuts, and beans. Lebanese food blends tempting mixes of mint, cardamon, paprika, pepper, olive oil, garlic, and lemon.

Roasted lamb is also the centerpiece of *mahrajans,* outdoor festivals sponsored by Lebanese American organizations. Many people of Lebanese heritage travel great distances to attend a mahrajan to see relatives and renew acquaintances. Hundreds of people gather in a park rented for the occasion to share a meal and enjoy Arabic music and dancing. While a lamb tied to a spit rotates over the coals, young men and women stand in a curved line, hold hands, and dance the *debkee.* The debkee is a folk dance that reminds many Americans of line dances. The group circles to the right while doing a synchronized step and kick. Dancers move to the beat of *derbekki,* ceramic drums with leather stretched across the tops, or to a tape of their favorite Lebanese singers.

Family meals in the home provide opportunities for more intimate visiting. Relatives or neighbors may drop in for late breakfasts on weekends, or the immediate family may gather for some leisurely discussion. Many Lebanese Americans have adopted American breakfasts of cereal, pancakes, or eggs and toast, but others also serve traditional Lebanese fare. A typical Lebanese breakfast may include olives, *jibnee* (a salty cheese), *zahter* (a mixture of thyme and sumac), and scrambled eggs sprinkled with *kamoun* (cumin). Everything is eaten with pita bread. Hot tea or coffee is served. For a heavier breakfast, Lebanese Americans may serve *fool,* a mixture of fava beans, onion, garlic, tomatoes, mint, lemon juice, and olive oil. Fool is scooped up with pita bread from a common dish. No meal is considered complete without bread, called "the staff of life" by Lebanese and others since biblical times.

Hospitality

Lebanese Americans are known for the generous hospitality they offer friends and strangers alike. And it is a trait they value highly in others. That is because, like other Arabs, they traditionally view hospitality as a sacred duty. Lebanese Americans trace the importance placed on hospitality to the Bedouins, nomads from the Arabian peninsula who came to what is modern-day Lebanon in the seventh century. Bedouins highly valued hospitality at a time when not welcoming a stranger for a meal and rest would likely mean the stranger's death because they were in the desert.

Sharing meals is one of many ways Lebanese Americans extend their hospitality. Other ways they demonstrate their hospitality include maintaining an open house, enthusiastically welcoming guests, generously sharing their time and possessions, and serving endless rounds of hot tea and coffee. Friends visit each other regularly and often come unexpectedly. When guests stop by spontaneously, a good host and hostess drop everything and entertain them.

Some families prepare a room of the house especially for entertaining guests. It is immaculately kept, always prepared for the unexpected arrival of friends. Guests are offered the most comfortable chairs. Then tea (called *shy*) or coffee is usually served, often without asking guests if they want it or not, as other Americans might. Lebanese Americans will show respect for age by serving the elder guests first. Sweets or fruits are also served to visitors. A favorite desert is *baklawa,* layers of thin pastry filled with sugar and nuts.

The serving of Turkish coffee is an important part of entertaining, but it must be done just right. In formal visits, particularly among new acquaintances, the time of the serving is significant. To honor the guest, it should come near the end of the visit. If the coffee is served too early, it might seem a hint for the guest to leave. If it is served too late, and the guest has already risen to go, it might seem like an afterthought. In either case, the guest might feel insulted. Some careful hosts serve coffee twice, calling the first serving the "welcome coffee," indicating clearly that the coffee carries no hint that they wish the guests would leave.

Besides the timing, the way Turkish coffee is served and received can signify mutual respect. Finely ground coffee should be boiled in water with sugar and cardamom, and the coffee should be offered to guests in demitasse (petite coffee cups and saucers used in France). Each cup should be full, but coffee should not reach the brim. A tray of chocolates and candies is often passed around while guests are drinking coffee. Everyone takes a piece or two. If they do not, their host will insist. Some Lebanese Americans serve one glass of water with a tray of coffee. Guests may choose to take a sip of water before drinking the coffee but not after. Some people interpret drinking water after having coffee as washing away the taste because the coffee was not good.

Coffee has been revered in the Middle East as a special beverage for centuries. After the Muslim prophet Mohammed said that Allah (God) prohibited the drinking of wine, some Muslims began calling coffee *"qahwah,"* an expression meaning the "wine of Araby." The traditional Arabic qahwah is not the thick Turkish coffee, but a thinner mixture of coffee and cardamon that is served without sugar. Serving Arabic coffee involves a ritual inherited from the Bedouin that a few Lebanese Americans continue practicing today. A small cup is poured for one guest. The host keeps refilling the cup until that guest indicates he or she has had enough by shaking the cup. Then a cup is served to the next guest. While Lebanese Americans more often serve Turkish coffee than traditional Arabic coffee, some serve the Arabic coffee on special occasions.

Even when they are not entertaining at home, Lebanese Americans often assume the role of host. If you are out to eat in a restaurant with Lebanese American friends, do not be surprised when they pick up the check and pay for everyone. Carefully calculating each person's tab and splitting the bill seems stingy to them. Besides, they enjoy getting together often and figure that if everyone is equally generous, eventually all will pay their fair share.

Lebanese Americans show similar generosity in responding to requests for favors. If asked to do something, even if it is something inconvenient or difficult, they will not offer excuses or bluntly refuse. If they cannot accommodate the request, they will at least make a token effort. To refuse to help a friend is viewed as a breach of loyalty. To fail in your effort to help is considered far better than not trying at all.

Being Polite — Lebanese Style

Being hospitable and generous are important ways Lebanese Americans express their respect for others. They also consider a number of other rules of etiquette essential for demonstrating respect. Among them is dressing properly for each occasion. When Chirrinne goes to school, she will often wear blue jeans and sweatshirts like her other classmates. But when she attends a party or celebration, she prefers to wear a fancy dress. Her Lebanese American hosts will interpret her choice of clothing as a sign of her respect for them and for the occasion.

Likewise, the way she stands or sits when talking with others is important. If she slouches or sits carelessly, especially with adults around, others may take offense. It is also taboo to allow the sole of your shoe to face another person.

In contrast to these rules of etiquette, the failure to arrive on time to a party or dinner is not always interpreted as a lack of respect. Although many Lebanese Americans are careful to arrive on time, others are not. Some view social occasions as having no fixed beginnings or endings. Consequently, they do not realize they might have kept you waiting or inconvenienced you, even when they arrive long after the festivities have begun. Likewise, many Lebanese American hosts are flexible with their plans and are not concerned about what time you actually arrive.

Like their views of time, Lebanese Americans also have a perspective on privacy that is different from that of other Americans. Topics many Americans feel are confidential are not for Lebanese Americans and others of Arab heritage. For example, many Arabs will ask you what you paid for things or how much money you make. Likewise, if someone is married and doesn't have children, a Lebanese American acquaintance would not hesitate to ask why.

Marking Life's Milestones

Lebanese Americans have many opportunities to demonstrate their good manners because all of life's milestones are celebrated with family gatherings and visits from friends. Birth, baptism for Christians, marriage, and death are all occasions for coming together to participate in age-old rituals that demonstrate the joy or sorrow of the occasion. Lebanese immigrants brought their rituals with them, and today's Lebanese Americans have kept them.

Birth. The birth or baptism of a new baby is a joyful occasion, marked by parties and visits. Some families celebrate with a party with relatives and friends in their homes. Others do not plan a party but welcome the many guests who drop by. When an infant is born or baptized, Lebanese Americans show respect for the new parents by paying them a visit and bringing gifts for the baby.

Marriage. The most elaborate celebration is the wedding. Although each faith has its own particular ceremony, Lebanese Americans share some common wedding traditions that come from their Arab heritage. Few Lebanese Americans include all these customs in their wedding celebrations; instead, they have developed their own family celebrations, mixing old traditions with new American customs they have adopted.

In a traditional Arab wedding celebration, both the bride's and the groom's families hold parties in their homes. Relatives, neighbors, and other friends gather in each place. Feasts of lamb and rice are served. Then the groom and his wedding party make a visit to the bride's home and bring her to his family's house. At the bride's home, there are usually many tears when she symbolically leaves her family.

The bride's family and friends join in the trip to the groom's home (or more commonly today, to a party at a hall sponsored by the groom's family). The participants make as much noise as they can, honking car horns or shouting to let everyone else know a wedding is taking place.

Once at the groom's party, each well-wisher in attendance greets the bride and groom. Then the pair is seated on a platform, where they watch as their guests dance and sing in their honor. Occasionally, the traditional cry of celebration, *"La, la, la, la . . . leeesh,"* is heard.

Sometimes the palms of the couple's hands are dyed orange with henna (the same natural dye that Lebanese women used long ago to

dye their hair). The couple's orange palms mark them as newlyweds. If the party is held at the groom's home, dough is placed above the door as a sign of prosperity. Instead of tossing a bouquet to guests, the bride will throw candy and money, which are also symbols of prosperity.

Guests do not usually bring gifts to the wedding. After the couple has returned from their honeymoon, friends and relatives bring gifts to their new home.

Death. Like weddings, Lebanese American funerals have become a mixture of Lebanese and American traditions. The Lebanese American funeral is a time for demonstrating the sadness all the participants feel for the loss of a loved one. The more traditional the funeral, the greater the expression of grief.

Debbie Herro, the wife of a Lebanese American, recalls her surprise at the overwhelming expression of grief the first time she attended a Lebanese American funeral. One of her husband's cousins had died. "On the evening of the day he died, all the relatives and

A Lebanese American girl sings while relatives listen. Lebanese Americans celebrate weddings, birthdays, anniversaries, and other occasions with singing and dancing.

friends met at his house. They all sat together and shared their memories of him. A meal was served. The older people ate first, then the adults. Lastly, the children.

"His wake was held the next day at a funeral home. I wasn't prepared for the wailers," says Debbie. Wailers — a small group of older women who knew the deceased well — set the tone for the funeral. They tell stories of the deceased, remembering the good things he or she did. They talk about how much he or she will be missed. They cry and chant and wail.

At the funeral service, held at a church, funeral home, or mosque, relatives and close friends of the deceased dress in black. (A spouse or a parent of the deceased sometimes dresses in black for the rest of his or her life.) For Christians, special liturgies are performed. Sometimes services are held in a church, but many families prefer graveside services.

During an Islamic funeral, special prayers are offered in the mosque by the *imam,* an Islamic clergyman, or by another member of the Muslim community who is a friend of the family of the deceased. Before or during the prayers, a special ritual washing of the body of the deceased is done by knowledgeable Muslims, and the body is wrapped in white muslin cloth and placed in a coffin. When the body is buried, the head of the deceased is placed toward the east, in the direction of Mecca, Saudi Arabia, a sacred Islamic site.

Immediate family members and, sometimes, other relatives refrain from pleasurable activities like watching television, listening to music, attending parties, and visiting restaurants for a time after a death. (How long depends on the individual.) Others in the community demonstrate their respect for the family in mourning by asking the family's permission to hold weddings or other celebrations in the year of that family's loss.

For Lebanese American Christians, the funeral ceremony is but one of a series of ceremonies for remembering the deceased. Relatives gather again forty days, one year, and two years after the death to commemorate their loved one. A requiem liturgy is performed at those ceremonies. Boiled wheat germ cooked with sugar and nuts (called *kilbee* or *ruhmee),* which symbolizes resurrection, is served. Sugar added to the wheat germ symbolizes the sweetness of everlasting life.

Lebanese Americans highly value these ceremonies. Care is taken that the proper traditions are observed so that the people being honored — whether for birth, baptism, marriage, or death — are shown the proper respect.

Arabic: A Language of Power and Identity

Just as important as knowing what to do and how to do it is knowing what to say and when to say it. The Arabic language, which is spoken by virtually everyone in Lebanon, has many blessings and polite expressions that are used in specific situations. For example, when someone buys something new, the polite reaction is to say *"Mabrook"* as a way of offering congratulations. The purchaser will respond *"Allah yibarik feek,"* which translates as "May God bless you." And saying *"shukran"*— which means "thank you" in Arabic — for favors and gifts is, of course, appreciated. The response is *"Afwan"* or *"Tukram"* ("You're welcome").

One reason Lebanese Americans and other Arab Americans place great stock in blessings and polite platitudes is that they traditionally believe words have power. When Christian Lebanese Americans leave on a trip or undertake a difficult or dangerous task, for instance, they often make the sign of the cross and say *"Be ism Il Ab, Wal Ibn, Wal Rooh Il Kodos,"* meaning "In the name of the Father, the Son, and the Holy Spirit." Likewise, Muslim Lebanese Americans in the same situations say *"Be ism Allah"* ("In the name of God"). Those bidding their friends a bon voyage, both Christian and Muslim, will say *"Allah koon ma'eck,"* translated as "May God be with you." These expressions are not simply good wishes. They confer a blessing that will help protect friends on a journey.

For Muslim Lebanese Americans, the Arabic language itself is holy. Arabic was, they believe, the language God used to communicate with their prophet Mohammed. The holy book of Islam, the Koran, is written in classical Arabic. The Koran cannot be translated because, Muslims hold, the Koran exists only in Arabic. Once its words are translated into another language, it ceases to be the Koran.

Although Lebanese Christians do not consider Arabic a sacred language, they, too, hold Arabic in great esteem. One's ability to speak eloquently and read and write formal Arabic is highly respected. They consider how you say something as important as what you have to say.

Consequently, Arabic is often spoken dramatically and loudly. If one speaks softly and makes a statement only once, a person of Arab heritage may question whether you actually mean what you say. Language scholars have noted that Arabic speakers tend to exaggerate and repeat their points. Some Lebanese Americans say that they repeat themselves because they often all talk at once and must repeat points to insure they were heard. They pepper their conversations with proverbs and flowery phrases. Discussions also tend to be loud, and onlookers may think the speakers are ready to come to blows, but most of this is done for dramatic effect.

The Arabic language is an important key to the Lebanese American identity. It is the basis of their Arab heritage and provides Arabic speakers with a sense of being one nation with other Arabic speakers, regardless of the existing national boundaries in the Middle East.

This is not to say Lebanese Americans do not feel stronger ties to Lebanon than, say, to Saudi Arabia or Egypt. Most Lebanese Americans are proud of Lebanon's distinctive cosmopolitan culture and modernity. But the Arabic language ties Lebanese Americans to others who speak Arabic. It provides a feeling of Arab brotherhood and sisterhood among Arabic speakers in the United States, the Middle East, North Africa, or anywhere else.

So when many second- and third-generation Lebanese Americans did not learn Arabic, they lost more than the ability to speak another language. Many historians point out that one reason the children of Lebanese immigrants assimilated so quickly and thoroughly into American culture is that many of them did not learn Arabic. In the 1920s, there was strong pressure on all immigrants, including the Lebanese, to Americanize. Lebanese-American children were encouraged to master English rather than Arabic. But with the loss of language came a loss of cultural heroes and folklore from their ancestral home. So like many other immigrants, they filled the void with American legends and heroes like cowboys and athletes. Consequently, their sense of ethnic identity weakened, and they started viewing themselves as Americans.

When later immigrants from Lebanon came after World War II, they brought a revival of interest in Arabic language and Lebanese culture to the Lebanese American community. Although most second- and third-generation Lebanese Americans identify strongly with American culture, they also have a growing appreciation of their Lebanese heritage.

Consumer advocate and lawyer Ralph Nader. Nader, who has spent his life fighting corporations and government powers on behalf of average Americans, is perhaps the best-known Lebanese American today.

CHAPTER SIX

CONTRIBUTIONS TO AMERICAN CULTURE

LETTING THEIR LIGHT SHINE

There are many accomplished Lebanese Americans we know simply as Americans, like consumer advocate Ralph Nader, longtime senior White House correspondent Helen Thomas, or the Clinton administration's secretary of health and human services, Donna Shalala. Doug Flutie, the 1984 Heisman Trophy winner, made his mark in the exclusively North American game of football. And radio celebrity Casey Kasem has one of the nation's most recognized voices and has become a fixture in American pop culture. We appreciate their contributions to U.S. society, but we do not recognize them for their Lebanese heritage.

Making a Contribution from the Start

One reason we think of these Americans simply as individuals rather than as Lebanese Americans is that they chose to pursue individual dreams rather than community goals. Yet even first-generation Lebanese Americans, who were less inclined to flock together than other immigrants, influenced the development of American culture in quiet but significant ways. Many of them set out on the open road and sought their fortunes as peddlers. Eventually, they settled down around the country and set up shop, becoming store keepers and business owners. In doing so, they played a role in knitting the nation together and shaping the national character.

While they were following their own stars, the Lebanese immigrant peddlers filled an important niche in American life at the turn of the century. At a time when shopping malls and mail-order catalogs, television, and even railroads did not exist in the country's many isolated communities, Lebanese peddlers brought the marketplace to these communities. They also carried news from place to place, giving the nation a sense of unity. In the early 1900s, the peddlers, with their trinkets, lace, and news from other parts of the country, were welcomed guests at many a farmhouse. Perhaps that is why today Lebanese peddlers, such as Ali Hakim in the musical *Oklahoma!,* are fondly remembered in America's folklore.

During the peak peddling years, from the turn of the century until World War I, Lebanese immigrant peddlers also played a valuable role in fostering growing U.S. industries. By distributing the products of small U.S. industries throughout the country, they helped the industries grow.

The extensive network the peddlers established also served U.S. export trade. The network included merchants in the Middle East who sent goods to suppliers in the United States and other countries. Those suppliers provided goods to Lebanese immigrant peddlers. During World War I, when the war cut Latin America off from European trade, the peddlers — supplied by warehouses in New York —

RALPH NADER: THE PEOPLE'S ADVOCATE

Ralph Nader made a name for himself as the champion of the powerless. He has spent his adult life fighting for the rights of average Americans against big corporations and government powers. The slim lawyer, who lives in a rooming house and does not even own a car, consults presidents and the U.S. Congress about the rights of consumers.

Nader, who graduated from Princeton University and Harvard Law School, is perhaps the most famous Lebanese American today. "No living American is responsible for more concrete improvement in the society we actually do inhabit than Ralph Nader," wrote *Washington Post* columnist Michael Kinsley. Walter Mondale, vice president in the Carter administration, called Nader "a man without parallel in American history." In 1971, a Gallup poll rated him the sixth most popular man in the world.

Since his 1965 publication of *Unsafe at Any Speed,* in which he condemned U.S. automobile manufacturers for selling cars they knew to be dangerous, Nader has been in the public arena, fighting for the rights of consumers. He has taken stands against pollution, fraud, and unsafe practices at atomic energy plants. He has advocated for health standards in food and medicine and safety standards on the job. His work has contributed to laws that make safer consumer products, including cars and food. Nader also played an instrumental role in the creation of the Environmental Protection Agency (EPA) and the Occupational Safety and Health Administration (OSHA) and the passage of the Freedom of Information Act.

Perhaps his most lasting legacy is his example as an activist. As the leader of the consumer-protection movement, he organized investigative teams of lawyers, consumer specialists, and students, called "Nader's Raiders," to serve as watchdogs of numerous companies, federal agencies, and the U.S. Congress.

Nader's drive to challenge injustice came from his father, Nathra, biographers say. Both Nathra and Nader's mother, Rose, came to the United States in 1925. They arrived in Newark, New Jersey, from Mount Lebanon. Nathra worked for one year there in a machine shop, then took to the open road as a peddler. The family settled down in Winsted, Connecticut, where Ralph Nader was born in 1934.

The Naders operated a restaurant and bakery that they considered a place for feeding the mind as well as the body. The lively discussions of politics and ethics that took place there daily are said to have shaped young Ralph into the people's advocate he is today.

headed south into Latin America. By the 1920s, Lebanese immigrant traders were in every country of South America, Asia, and Africa, as well as Australia, distributing products from both the United States and the Middle East.

As a natural complement to the trade network, some Lebanese immigrants helped foster the country's banking and finance businesses. The Faour brothers — George, Daniel, and Dominic — started the first Lebanese-owned bank in the United States in 1891. The bank, located on Washington Street in Manhattan, served as the main lender to the Lebanese American community in New York. It also became a lender to America's many new immigrant groups.

Lebanese Laborers

Other Lebanese immigrants helped build this country through their labor and frugality. Most Muslim Lebanese, who largely immigrated at the end of the peddler era (during and after World War I), and some Christian Lebanese went to work as laborers. With every intention of returning to Lebanon with fortunes for their families, these Lebanese immigrants worked hard and lived simply. They provided some of the backbone for the growing U.S. steel and iron industries during the country's prime years of industrial growth in the early years of the twentieth century. They also helped build the automobile industry in Detroit.

Lebanese Americans in Manhattan and New Jersey resurrected their silk industry, which had suffered from blight and competition with the Far East when they were in Lebanon. By 1924, there were twenty-five Lebanese silk factories in Paterson and West Hoboken, New Jersey.

Lebanese immigrants in New York also found a distinctive niche in the garment industry. They were the main manufacturers of kimonos, a fashionable garment in the 1920s, and of Madeira lace. And, in spite of the fact that Jews, their chief competitors, owned 97 percent of the garment factories at the time, Lebanese still made half the sweaters in New York. A Lebanese company, the N.P. and J. Trabulsi Company, was called the "king" of woolen knits.

Professional Children of Immigrants

Like their parents, the children of the Lebanese immigrants pursued individual goals. Many of them proved themselves through education and made their marks in medicine, law, and scholarship. Dr. Michael De Bakey is well

Actor Jamie Farr portrays Corporal Max Klinger in the TV series "M.A.S.H." Farr's character tried to get himself dismissed from the army by dressing in women's clothes. Like many children of Lebanese immigrants, Farr lived the American dream, finding success in his chosen profession.

known for his pioneering work in heart surgery at Baylor University in Houston. Dr. Elias Corey of Harvard University won the 1990 Nobel Prize for Chemistry.

Some became well-known entertainers. They include Jamie Farr (Corporal Max Klinger on the long-running TV series "M.A.S.H."), F. Murray Abraham (of *Amadeus,* winner of the 1985 Oscar for best actor), comedy actress Kathy Najimy (who appeared in *Sister Act* in 1992 and in *Sister Act II* in 1993), opera singer Rosalind Elias, singer-songwriter Paul Anka, and, of course, comedian, actor, and singer Danny Thomas and his daughter, Marlo, both of whom became stars with appeal across a wide range of ages and generations.

THAT GIRL: MARLO THOMAS

Marlo Thomas became known to most Americans as "That Girl," the star of a successful television comedy by the same name that ran from 1966 to 1970. Thomas played a single woman on her own, a college graduate who wanted to be an actress. The character, Thomas's creation, had an overprotective father who wanted her to marry and have a family. The show was a forerunner of other series about independent women, such as "Rhoda" and "The Mary Tyler Moore Show."

The sitcom's story paralleled Thomas's own life. After her graduation from the University of Southern California, Thomas moved out of her family's Beverly Hills home to pursue her acting career. Her celebrity father was Danny Thomas, shown here in 1955 (that's Marlo at the piano with Danny), who once described himself as "overprotective," said in his autobiography that, in his Lebanese heritage, "a daughter doesn't leave unless she's wearing a white veil and a ring on her finger." Danny Thomas is among America's most famous TV celebrities of all time. His series, called "Make Room for Daddy," lasted eleven years (from 1953 to 1964) and went into at least nine seasons of reruns.

Marlo became a star in her own right. In addition to her television series, Thomas has had a successful career on stage and in film. She received the Best Actress Emmy for "Nobody's Child," a made-for-TV movie in which she played a patient in a psychiatric facility who was released, went to college, and went back to become head of the institution. She also became a producer of films for both television and the big screen and is active in a number of social causes.

Thomas also promotes respect for cultural diversity. In 1974, she created an acclaimed children's book called *Free to Be . . . You and Me* and, in 1987, its sequel, *Free to Be . . . A Family*. The concept for *Free to Be . . . A Family* was developed into a television special. Children were chosen from New York and Moscow to participate. They were assigned pen pals and later met via satellite television. The show was well received and won an Emmy.

Lebanese American Soldiers

In addition to their impact on the home-front, many Lebanese Americans made their individual contributions to the defense of the country. During World War I, fifteen thousand Syrians (as Lebanese were called at the time) — or 7 percent of the Syrian-Lebanese American community (most of whom were Lebanese) — served in the U.S. military. Many registered themselves rather than waiting to be drafted. Lebanese American Ashad Hawie is said to be the most decorated Lebanese immigrant in the war. A member of the famed 42nd "Rainbow Division," 167th Alabama Infantry Regiment, Hawie received the Croix de Guerre from the French when he captured a German quartermaster sergeant who carried instructions from the High Command for a resupply of munitions. He also successfully led a grenade counterattack on the elite Prussian Guard. He fought at the Battle of Verdun, where more than half his company were killed, and at the pivotal Argonne Meuse battle. He received the Distinguished Service Cross from General John Pershing. In his own memoirs of the war, Hawie compares the march of Christmas 1917

KHALIL GIBRAN (1883-1931)

One of the best-known literary figures of Arab heritage is Lebanese American Kahlil Gibran. His popular series of prose poems, *The Prophet,* has been unchanged and continuously in print since it first appeared in 1923. Its text, which deals with love, beauty, life, and death, has proved to be meaningful to several generations of Americans.

Gibran immigrated from Lebanon to the United States in 1895, when he was twelve years old. His father's involvement in a local tax-collecting scandal drove his mother, Kamila, to leave the mountain town of Bisharri. She immigrated to the United States with her four children: Khalil, his two sisters, and his stepbrother. In Boston, Khalil's mother first supported her family by peddling lace throughout the Boston suburbs. After they saved some money, the family opened a small dry-goods store.

As a young poet and painter, Khalil quickly came to the attention of Boston's artistic and literary community. Later, he moved to Greenwich Village in New York, where he matured as an artist. Gibran wrote essays, poetry, and novels in both English and Arabic. His work gained tremendous popularity, and Gibran became a recognized leader of the Lebanese American community. He died from illness related to alcoholism on April 10, 1931.

At the height of his influence, Gibran participated in debates about the Americanization of immigrants, among other things. A champion of Americanization, Gibran believed becoming American and being Syrian (as Lebanese were called then) were not mutually exclusive. In a message titled "To Young Americans of Syrian Origin," published in the English-language *Syrian World,* Gibran wrote: "It is to stand before the towers of New York, Washington, Chicago, and San Francisco saying in your heart, 'I am the descendant of a people that builded Damascus, and Biblus, and Tyre and Sidon, and Antioch, and now I am here to build with you, and with a will.' It is to be proud of being an American, but it is also to be proud that your fathers and mothers came from a land upon which God laid his gracious hand and raised His messengers. Young Americans of Syrian origin, I believe in you."

to experiences in Mount Lebanon, saying, "When we reached our halting point in the valley of the Marne after six days on the march, my own feet were swollen and bloody, though snow and low temperatures were not new to one reared in the hills of Lebanon."

Lebanese American soldiers also distinguished themselves in World War II. America's first World War II flying ace was Lebanese American Colonel James Jabara of Wichita, Kansas. Jabara was one of about thirty thousands GIs of Arab lineage (most of them Lebanese Americans) who fought against Germany's Hitler, Italy's Mussolini, and Japan's Emperor Hirohito in World War II. Jabara was awarded two Distinguished Flying Crosses. He later served in the Korean War, shooting down fifteen Soviet-made MIGs. In 1950, Jabara was named by the Air Force Association as its most distinguished aviator.

At home, Lebanese Americans actively sold war bonds. The Syrian-Lebanese American community in Brooklyn was recognized by the U.S. Treasury Department for raising several million dollars for the war effort. George Hamid, the owner of Atlantic City's Million-Dollar Pier and Steel Pier, raised three hundred thousand dollars as chairman of the Army-Navy Emergency Relief Society.

Sharing a Heritage of Food, Faith, Honor

One reason we do not attribute the contributions of these individuals to Lebanese Americans is that, until recently, most Americans have not taken notice of Lebanese Americans as a group. Why? Maybe it is because their numbers have been relatively small. During the first wave of immigration from Lebanon (from the late 1870s to 1914), one hundred thousand Lebanese came to the United States, compared to millions from Europe. Conse-

quently, their contributions to U.S. culture have not always been obvious. But it doesn't take much looking to find them. They particularly left their marks in three areas. Everywhere the Lebanese went, they took with them their food, faith, and sense of honor.

Food. Anywhere you can find a sizeable group of Lebanese Americans — in New York, Toledo, Detroit, Birmingham, Chicago, Los Angeles, and many other American cities — you will also find a number of Middle Eastern restaurants. These restaurants have brought new flavors to the American palate: pine nuts and rice, cardamom and coffee, yogurt and garlic, to name a few. *Shishkabob* (skewers of meat and vegetables) and *baklawa* (a sweet dessert made from thin phyllo pastry layered with walnuts, cloves, and cinnamon and covered with a syrup of honey and lemon juice) were introduced to the United States, largely by Lebanese Americans, although other immigrants, like the Greeks, also brought them. The magic Lebanese Americans perform with grape leaves and lamb, many-hued rices, and eggplant have charmed America's taste buds. Now *hummus* (a creamy dip of blended chick peas, sesame seed paste, and lemon juice), *tabbouleh* (a salad of minced parsley and cracked wheat), and *felafel* (a deep-fried spicy bean croquette) have become familiar foods. Recipes for them appear in American cookbooks. Round loaves of pita bread, now common on grocery store shelves and American dinner tables alike, fill a variety of all-American uses: to make sandwiches, salad croutons, and even pizza crusts.

And *mezze* — an array of small appetizers served on miniature oval trays — is so popular that mainstream restaurants in Washington, New York, and Los Angeles list it among their regular hor d'oeuvres. A typical mezze would include hummus, felafel, stuffed grape leaves, flat meat pies, marinated shrimp, cheese

Dinner and drinks at a Lebanese restaurant. Lebanese restaurants across the country have made Middle Eastern food popular in the United States.

and spinach pie triangles, and small portions of a variety of salads. In other cities, mezze is found mainly in Middle Eastern restaurants, but it is also showing up in home entertaining across the country.

Lebanese Americans brought not only new tastes but also new attitudes about food. Cabbage and grape leaves, filled with rice, lamb, and spices, rolled and moistened with olive oil, serve both to abate hunger and as a center of celebration. Many Middle Eastern dishes take hours to prepare. Because few people would go to such trouble to cook for themselves, these dishes are obviously meant to be shared. Americans who visit Lebanese restaurants or who have adopted some Lebanese dishes as their own have learned the joy of sharing a meal in the Lebanese way, sometimes even from a common plate. Many Americans gather with family and friends to enjoy meals that were passed down in Lebanese families from generation to generation (some dating back to the land of

ancient Mesopotamia). Although these dishes fill the belly, they also serve as a symbol of unity for the diners. The Middle Eastern meal is as an occasion to share an evening together with family and friends. The benefit of such an occasion is particularly important at a time when the pace of American life threatens to make the family dinner a relic of the past.

Faith. Another aspect of American life Lebanese Americans have influenced is religion. Although most of the early Lebanese immigrants were Christian, many Lebanese Muslims have also made their way to the United States. By introducing the United States to Islam, Lebanese Muslim immigrants have significantly added to America's religions. The growth of Islam is evident in the increasing number of mosques found across the country. Some of the more elaborate mosques include one in Manhattan's Upper East Side, another mosque that accommodates two thousand near the campus of the University of Southern California, and an Islamic Center outside Toledo, Ohio. Today Islam is gaining status in mainstream America, as shown by the fact that the U.S. armed forces now includes an imam, a Muslim religious leader, among its clergy.

Honor. In addition to their religious faith, Lebanese Americans — Christians, Muslims, and Druze alike — brought with them a strong belief in the equality of people. This belief made them ready supporters of democracy and fighters against discrimination. Traditionally, they believe that all people, regardless of status, have value and should be treated with consideration. Because of the importance they place on a family's reputation, or honor, their battle against discrimination has focused on negative media stereotypes of Arab Americans and other ethnic groups. To fight against harmful Arab stereotypes, Lebanese Americans helped create the American Arab Anti-Discrimination Committee in 1980. The ADC is the largest Arab American organization in the United States today. It was the idea of two Lebanese Americans, former U.S. Senator James Abourezk and political science professor James Zogby. The committee has been a vigilant challenger of negative media images of Arabs and has spoken out against discrimination suffered by other minority groups in the United States, as well.

The Future

If current trends continue, the ethnic makeup of the United States will change dramatically. Demographers predict that by the end of the twenty-first century, Americans of solely white, European heritage will have become a minority. With that change, the Lebanese American community, and the Arab American community to which it belongs, will become more visible. And the more the United States sees of it, the more it will hear, as well. The Lebanese American community can be expected to have a growing role in influencing U.S. foreign policy toward the Middle East, as well as laws stateside.

Lebanese Americans will also continue to shape U.S. culture, particularly because the nation's interest in ethnic foods and customs is on the rise. But their influence on U.S. culture will be deeper than the superficial trimmings, felt in more important ways than just providing one more booth at an international fair. They will have a role in shaping our values.

ENGLISH WORDS THAT CAME FROM ARABIC

Many English words come from Arabic. The words demonstrate the influence Arabs have had on Western culture. That is because medieval European scholars drew heavily on Arabic source materials in various fields. For example, many words pertain to mathematics and the sciences. The number zero was created by Arab mathematicians who gave it the name *cipher,* a term that stands to this day.

A look at the Arabic source of a word helps explain its meaning. For example, the word *admiral* comes from the Arabic phrase *Amir al-bahr,* which translates as "king of the sea." The following is a list of familiar words that come from Arabic: admiral, alchemy, alcove, algebra, algorithm, alkali, almanac, amber, apricot, arsenal, artichoke, assassin, azimuth, cable, candy, carob, check, cipher, coffee, cotton, divan, drub, ginger, jasmine, lemon, muslin, nadir, sash, sesame, sherbet, spinach, sugar, syrup, tariff, and traffic.

LEBANESE AMERICANS IN PUBLIC SERVICE

Several Lebanese Americans have been particularly active in public service. Among them is Philip Habib, who became one of the most influential diplomats of his time.

Habib began his career in the foreign service in 1949 as the third secretary at the U.S. embassy in Canada. As he moved through numerous posts, he became known as the State Department's leading expert on Southeast Asia. Under presidents Nixon and Johnson, he was a key negotiator at the Paris peace talks that ended the Vietnam War. In 1974, as assistant secretary of state, he worked to improve the political and economic conditions in war-torn Laos and Cambodia.

Habib achieved the highest post open to career foreign-service officers in 1976 when President Gerald Ford appointed him under secretary of state for political affairs. He continued in that position during the Carter administration. Under Carter, Habib arranged the historic meeting between Egyptian president Anwar Sadat and Israeli prime minister Menachem Begin that produced the 1979 Camp David Peace accord. In 1981, President Ronald Reagan called on Habib to help negotiate a cease-fire across the Israeli-Lebanese border.

Like Habib, the Clinton administration's secretary of health and human services, Donna Shalala (pictured here), has a record of public service. Shalala is a Lebanese American from Cleveland. Before her appointment to the Cabinet position, Sha-

lala served as assistant secretary for policy development and research at the federal Department of Housing and Urban Development, president of Hunter College in New York City, governor of the American Stock Exchange, director of the National Women's Law Center, member of the Council on Foreign Relations, and chancellor of the University of Wisconsin–Madison.

A number of other Lebanese Americans have distinguished themselves in public service. James Abourezk (D-South Dakota), the son of a Lebanese peddler in South Dakota, became the first Lebanese American senator in 1978. Representative Mary Rose Oakar (D-Ohio), in 1977, became the first Lebanese American woman elected to the U.S. Congress. Former Senate Majority Leader George Mitchell (D-Maine) is also a Lebanese American.

That is because Lebanese Americans are joiners and have become involved in U.S. institutions at all levels, whether as members of local school boards, the Rotary Club, or the U.S. Congress. Through their involvement, their values will help shape our country's values as a whole. Their industry, frugality, love of family, respect for education and religion, and strong sense of morality will shine brighter than ever in the American mainstream.

CHRONOLOGY

2500 B.C. Phoenicians found their first settlements on the Mediterranean coast in what is now Lebanon.

64 B.C. Roman Emperor Pompey conquers Phoenicia and claims it for the Roman Empire.

A.D. 400s The Maronite Church forms when a group of Christians, following a monk named Maron, separate from the Syriac Church; Maronites move from Syria to Lebanon and establish their first church there in 749.

630 Arab Muslims bring Islam, one of the world's great monotheistic religions, to Lebanon; Lebanon remains part of the Islamic, or Arab, Empire until 1250.

1019 The Druze sect is established when a group of Shiite Muslims claim that the caliph al-Hakim is the incarnation of God.

1097-1200 Christian Crusaders from Europe occupy Lebanon and establish ties between the Maronites and Christians in the West.

1516 Ottoman Turks conquer the entire eastern Mediterranean coast and Lebanon becomes part of the Ottoman Empire's province of Syria.

1794 A group of Byzantine Catholics joins the Roman Catholic Church and is referred to as the Melkites (the Catholic Church was divided into the Roman and Byzantine churches in 1054).

1854 The first Lebanese immigrant, Antonios Bishallany, comes to the United States to pursue religious studies.

1858-1860 Civil war rages on Mount Lebanon between the Maronites and the Druze; ten thousand Maronites are killed.

1866 U.S. missionaries found the Syrian Protestant College in Beirut, later known as American University of Beirut.

1869 The Suez Canal opens, bringing Lebanon's silk industry competition from the Far East, which causes many Lebanese to suffer economic hardship.

1876 Lebanese merchants display their wares at the Philadelphia International Exposition of 1876 and, later, at the Chicago Fair of 1893 and the St. Louis Fair of 1906; merchants' stories of riches in America lead many young Lebanese men to immigrate to the United States with the goal of bringing wealth back home to their families.

1881-1925 The first wave of Lebanese immigration brings one hundred thousand Lebanese to the United States.

1890-1914 Peddling is the most popular occupation among early Lebanese immigrants.

1891 The first Lebanese-owned bank opens on Washington Street in New York City.

1892 The first Lebanese American newspaper, *Kawkah Amrika (The Star of America),* is published in New York.

1898 The influential Maronite newspaper *Al-Hoda (The Guidance)* begins publication in New York; the Eastern Orthodox newspaper *al-Gharb (Mirror of the West)* and the Druze newspaper *al-Bayan (The Explanation)* begin circulating at approximately the same time.

1910 The U.S. Immigration Department classifies Lebanese as "Asiatics" and denies their entry on the basis of race; some Lebanese immigrants take their cases to court and win the right to stay; the issue becomes moot when the Immigration Act of 1917 makes it illegal to deny someone immigrant status on the basis of race.

1914-1918	World War I temporarily slows immigration to the United States; blockades and confiscation of food supplies for the Ottoman military, along with forced conscription into the Ottoman army, cause starvation and suffering among the Lebanese.
1919	The first mosque, a Muslim place of worship, in the United States is built in Highland Park, Michigan.
1920	The state of Greater Lebanon is created under French mandate, establishing modern Lebanon's borders.
1921	New U.S. immigration laws set quotas on the number of immigrants allowed from each country, slowing immigration from Lebanon.
1923	Lebanese American poet and artist Kahlil Gibran publishes a best seller titled *The Prophet*.
1926	*Syrian World*, one of the first English magazines for Syrian-Lebanese Americans, is published.
1946	Lebanon is granted independence.
1950	Lebanese American flying ace James Jabara is named Air Force Association's most distinguished aviator.
1953	Lebanese American television star Danny Thomas begins his long-running series *Make Room for Daddy*.
1967	Immigration from Lebanon and other Arab states increases after a coalition of Arab countries lose the Six-Day War with Israel; the war also spurs feelings of Arab nationalism among Lebanese Americans.
1970	Lebanese American disc jockey Casey Kasem begins his popular radio show "America's Top Ten"; the show is still broadcast on more than one thousand radio stations around the world.
1975-1991	The Lebanese Civil War is fought between the Maronites and Muslims, but also involves Palestinians, Israelis, and Syrians; the war increases the flow of Lebanese immigrants to the United States — approximately 43,150 Lebanese immigrate during the war.
1978	James Abourezk, a Democrat from South Dakota, becomes the first Lebanese American elected to the U.S. Senate.
1980	Two Lebanese Americans begin the Arab Anti-Discrimination Committee, the largest Arab organization in the United States.
1985	Lebanese American actor F. Murray Abraham wins the Oscar for Best Actor for his role in *Amadeus*.
1990	Lebanese American Dr. Elias Cory wins the Nobel Prize for Chemistry.
1992	President-elect Bill Clinton appoints Lebanese American Donna Shalala to the Cabinet as secretary of health and human services.

GLOSSARY

Arabs	A people with their own language and culture who originated in the Arabian Peninsula but later scattered throughout the Middle East, North Africa, and other regions.
Arghileh	A water pipe.
Bedouin	An Arab nomad who lives in the desert.
Caliph	The political and religious head of an Islamic state.
Crusades	The military expeditions undertaken by European Christians in the eleventh, twelfth, and thirteenth centuries to capture the Holy Land (the parts of Lebanon, Palestine, and Syria where Christianity began) from the Muslims.

Discrimination	Treating a person differently because of sex, race, age, or any other characteristic of a particular group of people to which he or she belongs.
Druze	Followers of a religion that began as a sect of Islam in 1019 who believe that the caliph al-Hakim was the incarnation of God.
Eastern Orthodox Church	The branches of the Catholic Church that stem from the Byzantine tradition, which was formed when the Church split into the Roman and Byzantine churches in 1054.
Extended Family	Aunts, uncles, cousins, and all other blood relatives outside the nuclear family.
Greater Syria	A region established in ancient times by the Seleucids that included present-day Lebanon, Syria, Jordan, Israel, and Iraq; it became a province of the Roman Empire in 64 B.C. and a province of the Ottoman Empire in A.D. 1516.
Imam	A Muslim cleric, or member of the clergy.
Koran	The holy book of Islam that is believed to contain revelations made by God to the Muslim prophet Mohammed.
Lent	The forty days from Ash Wednesday until Easter that are observed by Christians as a season of fasting.
Maronites	Catholics who are part of the Roman Catholic Church but are distinguished by their unique liturgy and traditions.
Melkites	Catholics who were part of the Byzantine tradition but were persuaded by French missionaries in 1794 to join the Roman Catholic Church.
Mosque	A Muslim place of worship where community prayer services are held.
Muslims	Believers of Islam, one of the world's great monotheistic religions, which originated on the Arabian Peninsula in the seventh century with the teachings of the prophet Mohammed.
Patriarch	The elder male and leader of an extended family.
Ramadan	The ninth month of the Muslim year, which is based on a lunar calendar; during this month, which is honored as the month in which God revealed his message to the Muslim prophet Mohammed, Muslims fast from sunrise to sunset.
Stereotype	An overly simplified opinion or belief about a group of people.

FURTHER READING

Abinader, Elmaz. *Children of the Roojme: A Family Journal.* New York: W. W. Norton and Company, 1991.
Friedman, Thomas L. *From Beirut to Jerusalem.* New York: Farrar Straus Giroux, 1989.
Gumbley, Frances and Brian Redhead. *Pillars of Islam.* London: BBC Books, 1990.
Harik, Elsa Marston. *Lebanese in America.* Minneapolis: Lerner Publication Company, 1987.
Jomier, Jacques. *How to Understand Islam.* New York: Crossroad, 1989.
Mallon, Elias. *Neighbors: Muslims in North America.* Cincinnati: Friendship Press, 1989.
Marston, Elsa. *Lebanon: New Light in an Ancient Land.* New York: Dillon Press, 1994.
Naff, Alixa. *The Arab Americans.* New York: Chelsea House Publishers, 1988.
Orfalea, Gregory. *Before the Flames.* Austin: University of Texas Press, 1988.

INDEX

80